Sister to Sister

Sister to Sister

The 21 Day Devotional
You Didn't Know You Needed

Virginia Telamour

©2021 More Life Enterprises, LLC

All rights reserved. No portion of this book may be reproduced, stored in a retrieval system, or transmitted in any form or by means – electronic, mechanical, photocopy, recording, scanning, or other – except for brief quotations in critical reviews or articles, without prior written permission of the publisher.

Published by More Life Enterprises.

Unless otherwise noted, all Scripture quotations, are taken from the Holy Bible, New Living Translation. © 1996, 2004, 2007, 2015 by Tyndale House Foundation. Used by permission of Tyndale House Publishers, Inc., Carol Stream, Illinois 60188. All rights reserved.

Scripture quotations marked KJV are taken from the King James Version.

Song lyric excerpt: He Turned It – Tye Tribbett, Album: Great Than (LIVE)

Any Internet addresses, phone numbers, or company or product information printed in this book are offered as a resource and are not intended in any way to be or to imply an endorsement by More Life Enterprises, nor does More Life Enterprises vouch for the existence, content, or services of these sites, phone numbers, companies, or products beyond the life of this book.

Disclaimer:
Fasting is a personal decision that should be made at the discretion of the individual. If you have health concerns, or are under the care of a physician you are encouraged to consult with your medical professional prior to committing to fast.

Author Photographer, Cassidy Duhon - Duhon Photography

ISBN: 978-1-7378921-0-6

Table of Contents

Acknowledgments	7
Dedication	8
Foreword	9
Day 1: Seeking God	13
Day 2: Fasting	21
Day 3: Trusting God	27
Day 4: Faith	31
Day 5: Obedience	37
Day 6: Forgiveness	43
Day 7: Love	49
Day 8: Depression	53
Day 9: Self-Control	61
Day 10: Goal-Digger	65
Day 11: Fearlessness	71
Day 12: Positively Thinking	77
Day 13: Don't Stay Mad	83
Day 14: More Grace	89

Day 15: Less Worry	95
Day 16: Giving	103
Day 17: Wisdom	109
Day 18: My Body is a Temple	115
Day 19: It Might Be a Test	121
Day 20: I Am Light	127
Day 21: Freedom to Choose	133
About the Author	139

Acknowledgements

I'd like to thank my tribe for supporting my assignment, holding me accountable to it and encouraging me.

Thank you to my team:
Editor, (soon-to-be Minister) Laura J. Downey
Formatter, Meredith Bond of Anessa Books
Professional Coach, Rochelle Holness of Better Me

Dedication

This book is dedicated to Ms. Piggy My Sweet, mommy. Thank you for sharing the Lord with me and for making Him a nonnegotiable in my life. Thank you for your daily prayers, constant support, and innumerable sacrifices. God, I thank you for choosing her as the vessel to bring me into this world.

Foreword

I always knew I wanted to be an author but never imagined this. In 2016, I began reading devotionals regularly because I wanted to study the Word differently and take notes so I could later read and reflect on what I learned. As I read the devotionals, something struck me. I began to think about how I had not seen many devotionals that discussed topics relevant to the 21st century woman, like me.

Life for the 1980s woman as an adult is not the same as the 2000s woman—the now "modern" woman. With technology such as smartphones and social media, a lack of privacy both intentionally and unintentionally, I began to wonder where God fits into all of this. Yes, we declare that God is the center of our lives or God is sovereign, but how? How do I live a life that glorifies God daily and reflects Him as the center of my life? I believe distractions and trends have always existed but as time progresses, it's become more challenging to avoid those distractions and/or overcome them. Whether it is body image issues, professional success, personal success—whatever that may look like, we all at some point face challenges that we discuss freely with those who we trust. But what I was guilty of was a lack of proclamation for spiritual success; and that too, is a challenge.

See, we can go to church and profess, proclaim success in our homes, finances, careers, love lives, health, and our walk with God. We can go to work or just kick it with our friends at home, over dinner, on trips, and proclaim everything except our walk with God.

Think about it. When was the last time you told a friend, "I'm just trying to live right and do right by God" or "I want to be successful in God's eyes and by His standards?" See, there's nothing wrong with wanting and speaking life into the earlier topics, but there is something to be said about realizing success with God; though you say it in your prayers, you say it alone. Though you declare it at church—it isn't something you declare outside of church around believers and nonbelievers alike. Why is that?

I believe it is because we don't want the accountability that comes with those declarations. You say to your friends, I want to lose weight and sustain a healthy lifestyle; they encourage and support you by checking on you when you're having a serving that's for two people and not just the recommended one serving for one person.

Likewise, when you declare your desire to live a Christ-like life, there's pressure attached to it. But you have friends and even enemies that will be quick to call you out when you curse, compare yourself to others, and doubt who you are, etc.

I've done all of the above (and still struggle with some) but I wanted to change. I wanted the change to happen on the inside so it would reflect on the outside. So, I fasted and meditated on what I heard God saying to me. I wrote this book to help myself become the woman God designed me to be; a better version of who I was. I wanted reference points in one book that I could read to get clarity or encouragement on what God's Word says, because His Word, was, is, and will continue to be the highest standard.

Yes, the world is ever-changing and evolving and though God's Word does not change, His Spirit has revealed to me how I should be applying His Word in my life. I wanted to share this message with you. There aren't any tricks or gimmicks

Foreward

attached. This devotional is simply the Word we believers of Christ adhere to and it serves as a how-to please Him through our trusting of it.

I know you will be blessed. I want you to remember what you read. Meditate on it and then share it with another woman. That my sister is iron sharpening iron.

I love you and there's nothing you can do it about it!

Walk IN Love,

Virginia

Day 1
Seeking God

~Key Scripture~

Isaiah 45:19 📖 I publicly proclaim bold promises. I do not whisper obscurities in some dark corner. I would not have told the people of Israel to seek me if I could not be found. I, the Lord, speak only what is true and declare only what is right.

~Discussion~

We're told to seek God with the assurance that it will not be in vain; however, many of us find ourselves asking, "*How* do I seek Him?" "What should I be doing to seek God?"

Well, first, let's discuss what this means and how it looks. Seeking the Lord means we are seeking *His* presence. There are some who seem to maintain a constant relationship with Him. There are others who seek Him out of curiosity. For some of us, we seek God when we are in trouble. Sometimes we blame Him for what's happening, then eventually neglect, deny, and/or stop trusting Him. God doesn't want that for us, which is why He encourages us to seek His presence so we can stay connected to Him, *the Source.*

So then how do you seek Him? Well, believe it or not, the answer is easier than you think.

Close your eyes and imagine the dream job you desire. As you dwell on this, think about how you prepared and the research you did. What exactly did you do? You probably started with Google. Once you saw the resources and information out there, you started reading and scrutinizing every detail; it probably felt good, too. Eventually, you learned a lot and became hopeful that this dream was achievable; it could come true. You had a yearning; you were motivated and that pushed you more. It may have even become a *slight* obsession. You talked about this dream and wanted to know more. Remember that good, happy feeling of anticipation you felt on the inside during the process? How about the satisfaction when it actually manifested? Well friend, *this* is exactly how you seek God. And guess what? You get those same feelings but even better!

Your heavenly Father is asking for that same type of energy and attention from you. Not because He doesn't know you, but rather because He *does*. In fact, He knows you so well that He understands that you may not fully appreciate Him if He forces himself on you. So, He waits and allows you to choose Him, even though He's already chosen you. Your heavenly Father is a gentleman and although He wants you to desire Him, He doesn't bully His way into your life. But He might give you a nudge every now and again.

Why do we seek God? Well for starters, because God tells us to. I know, that sounds very cliché but let's not forget we were created to worship Him. So, this request isn't unreasonable or unrealistic. God isn't in the business of telling us to do things for the sake of doing it, even though He could. God always has a reason behind His commands, requests, and instructions. The problem is, a lot of times we don't know the reason or don't understand the purpose and value associated with His instruction, so our human response is to either not comply or

Day 1

give part-performance, which is essentially going through the motions. Perhaps if we knew the end from the beginning (like He does), we'd be obedient and give 110% the first time around, right? Because when we know the direct benefit, we suddenly feel like we can control the events that lead to our end goal.

We seek God because we recognize that He understands all things and is the answer to all things. God is the key. He is the Source. But He isn't going to just give you what you ask every time. Sometimes, He's going to make you earn it. Other times, He's going to lead you to it. But guess how you get that map and legend, that revelation, that "aha!?" You get it from seeking, communicating, meditating, and listening to God. I'm not saying to walk with an air of holiness and religiosity about yourself. Instead, I'm saying your heart and mind should be in a consistent flow of seeking God.

When you surrender your mind, your will follows suit and it is in that seeking, that God in-turn reveals himself to you in a way that is undeniable while answering you. But the secret no one really shares is that there is no concrete schedule for "seek and find" or "ask and answer" with God. Meaning, just because you sought God this morning, does not mean He will reveal the answer you requested that hour or even that day. Hashtag Patience—but that's a conversation for another day (see It Might Be a Test). While we know He is more than able to do so, I believe there are times when God is measuring us based on our consistency.

Let's look at this in the world of dating. Think about how you expect a man to be consistent, especially in the early stages. Now ask yourself, am I that consistent with God? I know I'm not and depending on your relationship with God or how the Spirit is moving within you, you may or may not feel some level of conviction here. Nevertheless, don't misinterpret *that* conviction as a means of lowering your expectations with dating. The point here is to remind you that God has feelings too and the way you may feel about how a man pursues you could very well be how He feels about your pursuit of Him. Don't beat yourself up right now. If you're reading this, you should actually feel hopeful and grateful because there's time! Friend, you can improve your relationship with God or develop one. All it takes is your commitment to consistency.

How do you seek God?

1) By studying His Word. You don't have to be a Bible scholar to study His Word. It starts with finding a translation that is easy for you to understand. There are many available; just be sure that it is an accurate translation of the Word and not just a word. I go between the New Living Translation (NLT) and the King James Version (KJV). Before attempting to read and study, I thank God for the freedom I have to read His word whenever and wherever I want.

Then I ask Him to give me three things:
- Wisdom to interpret His Word
- Knowledge to know His Word for myself and
- Understanding to apply His Word to my life every day

You can really start anywhere in the Bible or look up a topic that interests you. Devotionals are a great start to reading the Bible. One of the reasons why I enjoy devotionals is because they allow me to engage with the Word differently than just reading a chapter or two.

2) Prayer. You can seek God just by closing your eyes and hushing your mind. Then think about who God is in your life.

Day 1

Who He says He is and who you want Him to be in your life. Affirm those thoughts in your mind. Prayer doesn't have to be filled with words, just filled with sincerity. Remember, God knows your heart and wants *you* to share it with Him.

3) Listening to Christian music. Music is strong; powerful. Think about it, a song can transport you to your past revealing distant memories—good or bad; it can also inspire visualizations of your future. You can minister to God by giving Him a personal concert and serenading Him. Listening to the right music will connect you to His presence.

4) Listening to biblical sermons and teachings. You have the option of accessing them on your phone, computer, tablet, the radio or television. Next time you're looking for something to listen to, try finding a sermon. When you choose to listen, you are intentionally choosing to seek God.

5) If you haven't already, connect yourself with a Bible-based church. Preferably one where the pastor is as comfortable preaching about money, heaven, and blessings, as he is preaching about hell, because they are all real. Joining a church also enables you to tap into other opportunities and ways to seek and serve God.

Once you begin to seek God, you will see changes in your life. What's funny is that sometimes the people around you will see the change before you do. It's similar to losing or gaining weight; you don't always see it at first but those around you will notice. You can never obsess over God; He wants that from you and promises that it won't be in vain. So now that you have some starters on seeking God, which one will you commit yourself to trying? Take a moment and think about it.

～Additional Scriptures～

James 4:8
Matthew 6:33

～Prayer～

Dear God, thank you for your boldness. Your decision to love me daily is bold. Your decision to avail yourself to me is bold. I recognize that I can never do anything to earn your loyalty. I'm grateful to serve a living God who can be found and who hears and sees all. As you know, I struggle with seeking you. Sometimes I don't know how to find you or where to look for you. There are times when I don't even think I'm worthy of finding you or you caring enough to be present. I ask in the name of Jesus, my mediator, that you will reveal yourself to me in ways that I can understand. Grow me in you so that I can recognize when you are present and when I have distanced myself from you. Thank you for giving me the opportunity to get to know you and ultimately share you with those around me. As I seek you, I pray that you'll keep me rooted in your Word so that I will reflect you in all areas of my life. I thank you in advance for doing this and more, for your glory. In Jesus' name, Amen.

Reflection of the Day: How will you seek God today?

_____

_____

_____

_____

Day 1

Sister to Sister

Day 2
Fasting

~Key Scripture~

Ezra 8:23 📖 So we fasted and earnestly prayed that our God would take care of us, and He heard our prayer.

~Discussion~

What is fasting and why is it significant to believers? I grew up in a Christian home but had no recollection of fasting in our household as a child. Yes, we participated in prayer shut-ins at church and in homes but fasting was foreign to me. I wasn't introduced to fasting until my collegiate years. Perhaps you heard of fasting as it relates to getting blood work or even dieting, but that's not what I'm talking about here. The fast I'm referring to is a sacrificial act of self-control and complete reliance on God.

Fasting is a conscious decision to seek God by giving up what satisfies your flesh. It's an intentional commitment made by you to allow yourself to be stretched in ways unimaginable at first, so that the Holy Spirit can make itself at home. You are theoretically, putting your flesh to sleep, while simultaneously awakening the Holy Spirit. You are forcing your flesh to submit to the Holy Spirit, which already lives and dwells within you. That sounds quite impossible until you realize how very possible it is!

Why is fasting important? Well, now more than ever, it is so easy to get busy with the noise in the world that surrounds us. When you fast, you're quieting the noise. You're telling your flesh that it does not control you or your body; the Holy Spirit does.

Fasting is also a form of exercising your faith because you're demonstrating the Holy Spirit at work within you, sustaining you. The act of fasting is seen in both the Old and New Testaments; it's not unique to just one part of the Bible or one segment of believers.

In the Book of Daniel, we see two different instances where Daniel demonstrates his faith in God by going against the norm for 10 days and seeking God's guidance through fasting for 21 days. Moses fasted for 40 days and nights when God rewrote the Ten Commandments—laws that even to this day are observed by believers and many nonbelievers alike. After proclaiming God's protection over His people, Ezra and his fellow Israelites fasted before God for a safe journey and their prayer was answered. Queen Esther fasted for 3 days to seek God's favor regarding the enactment of a law that could have otherwise led to not only her death but all Jews living in the 127 provinces between India and Ethiopia. Jesus fasted for 40 days and nights and during this period, was tempted by the devil three times.

Fasting is significant for believers because it is one of the ways we get God's attention and are able to see Him work and move on our behalf. Fasting is personal—even when it is a group or corporate fast (like a church-wide fast at the start of a new year). When you make the decision to fast, you are participating in a personal experience with God. You're not simply telling Him you choose Him; you are showing Him that you choose Him.

Before I begin a fast, I do the following:

1) Decide on how many days. There have been times when the Spirit has led me to continue past the end date.

2) Think about why I am fasting. What's my motivation?

3) Start setting the atmosphere and preparing my mind for the experience.

So, what am I doing during the fast? I'm praying. I'm praying to God for myself—needs, wants, desires; my family; friends; my community; my country; stories and situations that I hear about, and yes, even my enemies. I'm using all that newfound free time that I have from not watching TV or surfing the web or social media and am reading the Word and meditating on it.

What I am not doing is advertising or publicly discussing my fast or the fact that I am fasting with anyone. In an effort to not signal something is up, I don't become a recluse. So, I'll meet up with friends for a happy hour or dinner and be mindful of what I'm having. If they ask me why I'm not having wine or a cocktail, I say I'm doing a cleanse and cutting certain things out for a bit and that's it. Because fasting is a form of cleansing that our bodies should regularly experience. But I want to be clear here, while I may refer to my fast to the public as a "cleanse" I understand it's not and I don't treat it as such either. However, please know that if you are fasting but not praying, *you* are actually doing a cleanse or participating in one of the many ways to diet.

Jesus expects us to fast and admonishes public declarations of fasting because again, it is supposed to be between you and God, your heavenly Father (see Matthew 6: 16-18). So if you're struggling with sticking to your fast, talk to God about it and ask Him for help.

You don't have to be a SUPER SAINT or super saved to fast. No one is measuring your fast. Oh, and you know something, you might have a rocky start, a stumbling middle, and a barely made it ending. The good news is that God is looking at your heart, is aware of your intention, and gives you grace when you don't meet your expectations for Him. Remember, fasting is personal—it's literally between you and God.

With that said, respect the fast that you are doing. Fasting should not be taken lightly. God is paying attention and His response or silence is directly connected to your actions. Don't fool yourself by thinking that going through the motions without being present in them will please God. Be mindful; God doesn't *need* our fasting and praying or praises. We need Him. He's made it clear that even rocks can cry out if we don't! Birds sing His praises daily. The oceans roar His greatness. The wind moves as He directs. So, God does not need your less than sincere sacrifice. But, when you do offer up that sincere sacrifice, worship, or praise, He sees it and is pleased, and acknowledges it by blessing you (see Isaiah 58: 8-9).

Fasting can really deliver some great results in your life if you fully commit to it. It's not relegated to an "at-home" or "at-church" experience. Fasting is an everywhere-I-go mindset that makes you more aware of God's presence and sensitive to His promptings in your life. So be present and enjoy it!

~Additional Scriptures~

Isaiah 58:4-5
Daniel 1:8-15
Daniel 10:3
Exodus 34:28
Ezra 8:21-23

~Prayer~

Dear God, thank you for this new understanding of what it means to fast. I must admit, this seems like an undertaking that I might not successfully complete, but I want to try it because I want to draw closer to you. You already know how flawed I am and I'm grateful that even in my flaws you see value and purpose. As I prepare my heart and mind to fast, I ask that you tell me what to let go of and what to set aside so that I will not have any distractions blocking me from your presence. I trust you will grow me and stretch me during this fast. If I grow weak or frustrated, please give me the support and encouragement I need to continue with my fast. You know why I'm fasting and what my needs are. I pray that in the end, I will have multiple stories to share with believers and nonbelievers about how you moved in my life during my fast. I look forward to being an encourager to others who will make this commitment and I thank you in advance for meeting me where I am. In Jesus' name I pray, Amen.

Reflection of the Day: Do your desires align with God's will for your life?

_____

_____

_____

Sister to Sister

Day 3
Trusting God

~ Key Scripture ~

Isaiah 26:4 📖 Trust in the Lord always, for the Lord God is the eternal Rock.

~ Discussion ~

Let's face it, by now you've had at least one person betray your trust and that left you feeling embarrassed, stupid, gullible, and maybe even jaded. Unfortunately, for many of us, the more our trust is violated, the less we are willing to expose ourselves to future disappointment. That's normal and expected. It's called self-preservation. However, a new behavior emerges as a result of this violation. We begin to associate doubt with the one(s) who betrayed our trust *and* with new people, those who don't even have a track record with us. What's worse is, we categorize our heavenly Father, who is unlike everything and everyone in our lives, as being like our violator(s); despite the fact that He was, is, and will forever remain, consistent and unchanging.

Many times, we bring our concerns to the Lord in prayer, but we're not always sincere or operating in a place of genuine commitment toward God, because we're still dwelling in our earlier disappointments. It's unfortunate because if we're being honest with ourselves, God hasn't given us a reason to treat Him the way we sometimes do. Despite this, our Lord tells us that He will rescue us for His sake. Oftentimes, we find ourselves questioning the current state of affairs and feel abandoned or forgotten by God but the truth is, He has never forgotten us; not even when we're in our lowest place. God has your name and mine written on the palms of His hands. He tells us that even if it were possible for a mother to forget her child, He would not forget us, his darling children. Imagine that! What mother forgets about a child she gave birth to or lost? Hard to imagine, right? And God says that He won't forget about you or me and I choose to believe that.

So how do you repair your personal issues with trust or doubt when it comes to God? You challenge yourself. What is the worst thing that could happen when you trust God? Hmm... He doesn't give you *your* want? Well, if you've lived a little, I think you can reference a couple of times where a prayer wasn't answered, and *that* was the blessing in and of itself. You will never lose when you put your trust in the author of your story.

What about people? Trust is a necessary component in relationships and friendships. What do you do with that struggle? How do you handle it? By trusting the Spirit of God that lives within you! You see, all roads begin and end with God. It's that still, small voice that always has an opinion about something going on in your life or around you. That voice, the intuition, or gut feeling is how you acknowledge the Holy Spirit living in you. As a woman, we tend to want to give people the benefit of the doubt and sometimes to our detriment, ignore the voice that offers us unsolicited advice. I encourage you to lean into that voice. You'll know it is the voice of God because you've been speaking to Him and seeking Him. Here's an amazingly generous act of God though, even when you aren't seeking Him as much as you know you should, He cares for you enough to still ensure that the Holy Spirit speaks to you. So next time, stop and listen.

∼Additional Scriptures∼

Proverbs 3:5
Lamentations 3:25
Isaiah 49:15-16
Isaiah 48:11

∼Prayer∼

Dear God, thank you for your faithfulness. Sometimes because of the hurt and pain I've experienced, I forget that you are not like those who caused me pain. You are God. You are unchanging, kind, loving, and the most consistent presence in my life. Today, I ask you to remind me of who you are when I begin to doubt you. Please, don't hold my flaws and short memory of your goodness against me. Continue to strengthen my faith and trust in you. Allow me to hear your voice and recognize it clearly when I need your guidance. If I'm struggling with trusting you and the people you bring in or remove from my life, I ask that you give me confirmation so I will know it is your move and not my doing. I want to be in your will no matter the cost. I love you and am grateful for how you care for my heart, soul, spirit, mind, and body. I pray this in the name of your son and my Savior, Jesus Christ. Amen.

Reflection of the Day: What small step can you take today to show God that you trust Him?

_____

_____

Sister to Sister

Day 4

Faith

~Key Scripture~

Hebrews 11:1 📖 Faith shows the reality of what we hope for; it is the evidence of things we cannot see.

~Discussion~

You've probably heard the saying, "All you need is a little faith," which is a derivative of the scripture, "If you have faith the size of a mustard seed, you shall say to this mountain, move and it shall be moved." Have you ever seen a mustard seed? It's smaller than a peppercorn.

Our heavenly Father is so gracious that He tells us to simply have faith in His ability to deliver what we ask for and we in turn get to see the manifestation. Oftentimes, we get caught up in "faith the size of a mustard seed" that we miss the necessary ingredient: faith. I find it interesting that God uses the mustard seed as a visual aid for how much faith we should have. I think the visual aid serves a two-fold purpose. For one, it reveals to us that it doesn't matter *how* much we believe, so long as we believe. And it also lets us know that He is more interested in tapping into our potential. Yes, a mustard seed is tiny in your hand, but have you seen it after it's been planted and fully grown? A mustard tree can grow 25 feet tall with branches spread out to 20 feet. I'll let you think about that for a minute.

So, what is this faith that God requires of us? Well, the Hebrew word for faith is Emunah. Emunah means to take firm action; to believe in, trust in, and rely on God. Meaning, you take action that is unyielding and aimed at what you're believing God for. This action becomes the demonstration God wants to see from you, showing him that you believe in His ability. As a result of your demonstration, God's move is now activated and you get the reaction or response to your faith, from Him.

In 2017, I was living with a relative and was working with a temp agency in hopes of getting placed somewhere with competitive pay and the option of permanent employment. I interviewed for a position with this financial company, and I knew I'd be a good fit. They liked me and wanted to place me in another department. I entered the interview with one position in mind and left with an offer and a start date for another position, which at the time, was not even advertised. I was excited and submitted all my paperwork to avoid any delay with my start date. I was ready to join a new team and guess what? They went silent—radio silent. I didn't hear back from them and my agency had zero updates. Though it was out of my hands, I wasn't as nervous as I would've been in the past because I knew it was in my Father's hands. I trusted Him. But as the days turned to weeks, concern started to creep in, and anxiety was beginning to create a dialogue in my mind. This was because I had already created a budget and move-out date based solely on this "expected" first check. I decided to have a conversation with my Father and like a child, reminded Him of my needs and wants *and* what He said He would do for me. After all, the company had everything they needed from me and gave me a start date. Then, the Holy Spirit spoke

Day 4

to me and gave me a bizarre idea, something I'd describe as "crazy" faith. I decided I was going to take firm action, show up to the office, and hope God beats me there. No, I did not call the agency or the company before driving 40 minutes to the office. I told God my plan and let Him know that even if He didn't allow me to start that day, I would continue to trust Him and rest in comfort knowing that He has another, better door opened for me.

So, I showed up unannounced thinking, worst case, they'll send me home because they're still not ready for me. Best case, they'll let me stay. What I knew though, is that I needed to start that job on *this* new pay period. Although they were not expecting to see me that Monday, to my surprise, they expected me to begin sometime that week. Turns out, their headquarters approved my hiring the week before and notified them. The company then emailed my liaison at the agency, who did not see the email until Monday morning. When I showed up early on that day, my new supervisor invited me to stay because they were on-boarding two other new hires. They went ahead and added me to the group, and I ended up starting that day.

I had never done something like that before in my life. I share this story because it was the first time I tried my faith in that way. I committed myself to an act that could've been embarrassing and or disappointing, but I was willing to risk it and trust in God. God saw my action, my heart, my commitment, and reliance on Him and He responded to my FAITH.

So, what firm action do you need to take today? What situation have you been praying for and asking God to change? What have you done to show God you're willing to risk it all for Him? That's what faith is. It's not simply saying you believe or that you are just thinking about it. Faith is found in the doing. Remember, your doing is what triggers the ripple effect leading to your answer and ultimate victory.

~Additional Scriptures~

Hebrews 11:6
Matthew 21:22
James 2: 14-26

~Prayer~

Dear God, thank you! Thank you for explaining what it is you want from me and how I can give it to you. I'm also thankful because based on your request of faith—the size of a mustard seed—I understand that you will meet me where I am but first, I have to make a move. I ask that in the coming days, weeks, and months ahead, you'll give me opportunities to demonstrate my faith in you and grow in it. While I know I can start with mustard seed faith, I'd like to eventually get to a place where my faith encourages, inspires, and leads others to you. I'll admit right now, as you already know, I may be a little shaky at this, but I trust you. Remind me that if I don't see your manifestation, it could be because I haven't done my part. Remind me Lord that when I move, you will move. Allow me to do my part, so that you can do your part. In Jesus' name, Amen.

Reflection of the Day: Today, I challenge you to try God by doing something that aligns with what you've been praying for. If you don't know what you should do, start by asking the Holy Spirit. Then, be prepared to act boldly like it's already yours!

Day 4

Sister to Sister

Day 5
Obedience

~Key Scripture~

1 Samuel 15:22 📖 "What is more pleasing to the Lord: your burnt offerings and sacrifices or your obedience to His voice? Listen! Obedience is better than sacrifice, and submission is better than offering the fat of rams."

~Discussion~

Samuel's question to Saul is one that remains just as relevant to believers today, as it did before Christ's arrival in 1037 B.C. This inquiry is one that requires our own personal and truthful self-assessment and reflection.

When I think of the word obedience, I am naturally drawn to another word, steadfastness. Being steadfast means unwavering, loyal, resolute. This is because God requires us to be loyal to Him, unwavering of His standards for our living and resolute in our commitment to follow Him. When we have a steadfast mentality and Christ-like character, it becomes hard to be disobedient to God's word. This is because like obedience, steadfastness is a choice. One that we have free will to make even when the surrounding circumstances do not appear to be favorable.

Listen, our heavenly Father is not looking for believers to obey His word when it's convenient for them; anyone can do that.

What should set us apart from everyone else is our firm commitment to His Word when in public view and in private. We weren't made to be followers but rather leaders. You may not realize this, but we lead others to Him through our actions. These actions will either reflect our obedience or disobedience to His Word. OUCH! Does this mean that your disobedience could be turning both nonbelievers and new believers away? Absolutely, but God is gracious enough to give us time to repent and be corrected by Him.

What does obedience look like today? Well, the same as it did before Christ arrived on the scene. Loving our neighbor as we love ourselves, resisting the desires of our flesh by exercising self-control, and controlling what we say, being mindful of our temper, thoughts, and actions. These are just a few but, you get the point.

Yes, our heavenly Father requires a lot from us but if you pay close attention, you'll discover that His requirements are rooted in love.

Do we sin when we disobey God? Yes. But guess what? God is full of mercy and will forgive us every time. We just have to ask.

I once heard a preacher say, "You don't have to understand to obey." What does this mean? Well, practically speaking, it's the sign you see at the red light that says, "No turn on red." You're in the right-hand lane and any other time that turn would be legal; so why can't you turn right at this particular light? Well, you don't know but guess what, if you see a police officer around, you obey that sign because you don't want a traffic ticket. And what if you don't see the officer because he's hiding, waiting to catch you 'disobeying' that law so he can pull you over? What's more plausible though is that the sign is there to protect you from a collision you wouldn't see or anticipate. I imagine God's commands to us come from this place. God isn't like the police officer; He's different. While He is omnipresent and watching you blatantly disobey Him, He is also merciful and ready to forgive you for that sin. Now, that's not to say that you won't reap the consequences of your disobedience because we already know that for every action, there is a reaction or consequence.

God speaks to us and He shares who He is with us. Though His ways are mysterious to us, He is not a hidden God. He commands us to do some things and not do other things. Because we can't see the entire picture, we tend to use our human logic to justify our behavior when we should've been using our spiritual discipline to accept and obey His way. It sounds more challenging than it actually is. But next time you're faced with the opportunity to obey, ask yourself, "What's the worst thing that could happen if I do His will?" God will never lead you astray or down a path where He won't accompany you. You've probably told Him how much you love Him but if you want to *show* Him that you love Him, try obeying His Word.

∽Additional Scriptures∽

Psalms 40:8
Psalms 5:8
Proverbs 10:23
Isaiah 46:12-13
Isaiah 48:18
Luke 6:49

 Prayer

Dear God, thank you for being so patient with me. When I think of how patient or impatient I can be with my friends, family, loved ones, and strangers, it amazes me to see how your love for me slows your anger toward me when I disobey you. Today, I confess my sins to you. I confess that I haven't always listened to you and at times when I said I would obey, I turned around and disobeyed. I don't want to be that person. I want to be reliable. I want to be trustworthy. I want you to see me and know you can count on me to live as you desire and do as you say. I want my obedience to you, to be the light that others see and are drawn to. I'm grateful that you haven't given up on me and ask you to help me in my day-to-day life decisions. Help me to follow your lead and obey your commands, no matter what. If and when the enemy tries to intimidate me into disobedience, I pray that your Holy Spirit will step in and remind me who I am and whose I am. I am a child of the Most High God, the Creator of the universe, the true and living God. Your Holy Spirit enables me to do your will because greater is He that is in me than he that is in the world. I thank you for this and more. Be glorified in Jesus' name, Amen.

Reflection of the Day: You're not too far gone for God to use you. Take one step in His direction and watch what He does.

___

___

___

___

Day 5

Sister to Sister

Day 6

Forgiveness

∽Key Scripture∾

Matthew 18:21-22 📖 Then Peter came to Him and asked, "Lord, how often should I forgive someone who sins against me? Seven times?" Jesus replies: "No, not seven times, but seventy times seven!"

∽Discussion∾

When was the last time you said, "I'm sorry" to someone? Do you find it difficult to seek forgiveness? I know I used to. There was a time where I could not stand the thought of apologizing especially if I knew I was not at fault. I didn't care if I offended or hurt people with my direct responses or unsolicited opinions. I didn't understand forgiveness and was acting like your typical hypocritical Christian. Then something changed in me. I can't pinpoint the incident. I only remember telling myself to check my judgment level. It turns out that my predisposition to always judge made me think I was better than others in some instances and couldn't possibly need forgiving because I spoke the truth. What I didn't realize was that the truth was almost always lost in the delivery, *my* delivery. The irony is that at some point in the day, I'd turn around and ask God to forgive me of *all* my sins. Then wisdom would speak to me and give me a gut check. How can God take your plea for forgiveness seriously when you're out here—be it intentionally or not, hurting people with your words; actions;

inactions; ignoring them; and not asking them to forgive you? How can you knowing all this, turn around and ask God about forgiveness?

So I began thinking more about my responses to people and situations and my delivery. I paid special attention to nonverbal cues and body language because I understood that everyone wasn't vocal. And if I felt like I may have offended someone, I apologized. My intent wasn't to hurt or tear down a person. Because that is my truth, it made it easier for me to self-reflect on past conversations and interactions, see my fault, and apologize. Now, I believe I over-apologize. Seriously, sometime between 2016 and 2017, I went on an apology tour, just trying to clear the air. Imagine a world where people apologized more than they did not. How can you genuinely expect God to forgive you for telling a lie or disappointing Him, but you can't forgive those around you for the same things?

Forgiveness doesn't happen overnight. How do you know if you haven't forgiven someone? Well, one way I can tell is when my heart sinks and the weight shifts to the pit of my stomach. Suddenly thoughts of what hurt me come to the forefront of my mind and my heart is in shambles.

God can make all of those feelings go away but you have to ask for His help. When you ask for His help, reconcile in your mind that you will and do forgive that person. If you have to repeat that statement to yourself until you believe it, by all means, do that. Once you've committed to that decision, include them in your prayer. Speak sincerely to your heavenly Father about that person and do not curse them.

The Word instructs us to bless our enemies. So if the opportunity presents itself for you to speak ill of that person, you must choose to go against what may be a natural inclination to do and instead speak well of them or say nothing at all. Don't let your mouth dig your hole by taking on a role that is against God's will. Don't allow yourself to dwell on that person or participate in negative talk about them. Speak kindly of that person, wish them well, and stop reliving your hurt by recalling what caused it. When you find yourself struggling to do any of these, ask God for help. Remember, He makes you strong in your place of weakness. Speak forgiveness into reality.

Can you just imagine if God made forgiving us as difficult as we sometimes make it for others? Think about it, God doesn't tell us to ask for forgiveness over and over nor does He owe it to us, but His love... He doesn't tell us to beg for forgiveness or even mercy for that matter. Even before Christ, believers had to follow meticulous rituals in order to be forgiven. And we often saw sincere demonstrations of repentance.

God then made it even easier. Despite our DNA, being preconditioned to sin thanks to our ancestors, Adam and Eve, God forgives us every single time. We confess, repent, and God tosses our shame, guilt, and sin away into the Sea of Forgetfulness. Yet, we, who do not hold the power to create a universe much less turn the day into night, require more effort and demonstration from our brothers and sisters, than our heavenly Father. Is that more like God or less like Him?

ꙮAdditional Scripturesꙮ

Colossians 3:13
2 Corinthians 12:9
Luke 6:28
Proverbs 17:9

Prayer

Dear God, thank you for continuing to bless me with the gift of life. Thank you for your patience with me and constant forgiveness of my sins. I confess I have dimmed your light in my life through my unforgiveness. I know this is wrong and no longer want to be that believer who seeks your forgiveness but withholds it from my brothers and sisters. Help me Lord. I want to forgive and need the weight of unforgiveness that's currently sinking my heart at the thought of _____ to be relieved and eliminated. Release me from the hurt, pain, anger, envy, jealousy, and all other spirits that have kept me from seeking the forgiveness of those whom I've hurt. Help me to receive their forgiveness of my actions as well. Enable me to forgive those who have wronged me so that my spirit can be at peace with you. Lord, please use your strength in my weakness so that I may become more like you, daily. Thank you for your abundant grace, in Jesus' name, Amen.

Reflection of the Day: Who do you owe an apology?

_____

_____

_____

_____

_____

_____

_____

Day 6

Sister to Sister

Day 7
Love

~Key Scripture~

1 John 4:20(b) 📖 for if we don't love people we can see, how can we love God, whom we cannot see?

~Discussion~

You've probably heard the saying, "God is love," and it probably sounds cliché but, guess what, that's actual scripture.

I can't tell you 'how' to love God because that looks different for each of us but, I can share with you how to demonstrate your love for Him. I can tell whether or not you love Him by observing how you love others. This is what God is saying to us through 1 John in the key scripture. See, it's easy for us to love our family member who we admire or respect. Likewise, it is easy for us to love our friends because we chose them and have decided to nurture those friendships. However, God doesn't call us to do what is easy or comes natural in this regard because that's a given. He calls us to love our neighbors and love our enemies. Don't believe me, *see* Matthew 5:44, where Jesus not only affirms the command given by God in Leviticus 19:18 but also clearly commands us to love our enemies.

Why are we called to love our enemies? Note, scripture doesn't say to like them, but rather love. Why is that? I believe it's because we're not meant to like what is contrary to God; that goes for what we see in the world and, if we're being honest, what we see in ourselves. However, that dislike shouldn't translate to hate because hate leads to sin.

This means as a believer, you will see people, even fellow believers and nonbelievers who will live a life that contradicts God's Word. Some will be audacious without fear or regard for consequences while others will be unanticipated—perhaps shocking and disappointing. Nevertheless, as believers, we are called to love them all alike because that active demonstration reveals our love for God. See, we can never compare ourselves to God but imagine this Holy being, ever-righteous creator, seeing us, *His* creation constantly drop the ball. Imagine the God you serve hating you? Can you imagine what that would look like or even feel like? The thought of that literally scares me and clenches my heart. So, if you remember all of your personal wrongdoings that have not been publicized for the world to see or know, if you remember all the mistakes you've made during your journey through life and are aware of the lives you've impacted in a hurtful way, yet God still continues to love you unconditionally, how can you then turn around and hate another human being? What exactly makes *you* so special? What makes you the exception to a command that He gave so clearly without the need for interpretation?

Loving God is seen when you extend grace to your enemy. Because that shame they feel, it leads to their repentance, and glorifies God. Your sincerity in that grace reveals God's love in you to others.

When you choose to love your enemies, you're also choosing to reflect God's love and His presence in your life because it is that love which fuels mercy. And we can't get tired of being merciful toward others because God hasn't stopped nor has

He become exhausted of being merciful toward us. And we know this because He hasn't stopped the sun from rising on evildoers and allowed it to only rise for do-gooders. No, Matthew 5:45 tells us that He gives sunlight to both the evil and the good, and He sends rain on the just and the unjust alike.

So today, I want to challenge you to do something that wouldn't come "naturally" to your flesh. This requires you to tap into yourself and into the Holy Spirit. If there is anyone in your life that you hate, pray for them. Ask God to reveal where you lack in demonstrating your love for Him.

Additional Scriptures

Colossians 3:14
1 John 4:16(b)

Prayer

Dear God, thank you for loving me unconditionally, as flawed as I am. Please forgive me for professing my love to you, while living like I hate you. Please, show me where I can improve in loving you. Make me aware of my biases and give me opportunities daily to demonstrate my love for you through kindness and compassion toward others. I pray that where my flesh struggles with this type of love, that your Holy Spirit, will dominate and invoke your righteous love. Thank you in advance for doing this and so much more in my life, for your glory. In Jesus' name I pray, Amen.

Reflection of the Day: Do your day-to-day activities show God's love?

Sister to Sister

Day 8
Depression

~Key Scripture~

Romans 12:2 📖 Don't copy the behaviors and customs of this world, but let God transform you into a new person by changing the way you think. Then you will learn to know God's will for you, which is good and pleasing and perfect.

~Discussion~

I wouldn't be allowing God to fully use me if I weren't transparent with you about this topic. When I started writing this book almost 4 years ago, I was in a great place mentally, spiritually, and emotionally. Then about a month later, I received unexpected news. It wasn't good news and it left me feeling discouraged and defeated. I couldn't understand how or why everything I viewed as progress (because I was looking through the lens of hope) managed to actually be a derailment. It's not to say I had never experienced disappointment or encountered roadblocks; *that* was the story of my life. But it was different this time.

As I began to think of how the timing was inconvenient, money was lost, offers rescinded, I couldn't help but sink into a place of depression. Hopelessness will have you depressed. The thoughts wrecked my mind and spirit. I thought about how I couldn't share my story and feelings with my core group of girlfriends because they'd see me as I saw myself, a failure. It frustrated me because I was back on track with God and boldly proclaiming His Word and promises over my life. Yet, He was allowing this to happen. It made me feel like they wouldn't take Him or His promises to me seriously. But it wasn't my job to worry about how they viewed Him. It hurt me because I felt like I was continuing to let my mother down, failing her yet again. I sank lower with every thought and the enemy was right there 'supporting' me. I decided to isolate myself but it was strategic. I pulled away from a couple of friends completely, and occasionally spoke to others. I updated my social media pages to avoid any red flags but the reality was that I was in a dark place.

I can recall getting ready to board a flight one day and selfishly asking God to just kill me. I wanted to die. No, not figuratively, but like in a swift accident; go to sleep and never wake up. I couldn't bear to see myself and the loser I had become. I hated me. I didn't denounce God. I didn't explicitly reject Him, but me wishing death over myself, was an implicit rejection. I had some words for God. I kept asking, when will my time come around? When will I be led out of the wilderness? How much more humbled can I become? My heart was heavy. I went to church and my pastor didn't see the pain in my eyes. No one on earth cared and my heavenly Father was just watching on the sidelines. I thought about taking pills, but then I thought of how much more ashamed and embarrassed I'd be if it didn't work.

Then suddenly one day, something changed. I can't tell you *what* began to change, but I know it was a feeling, and it wasn't my doing. Maybe it was the unknown prayers of others coming through. I was still in a dark and lonely place but God's spirit wouldn't give up on me. I found myself visiting a church on a Tuesday evening and the guest preacher said

Day 8

something that resonated with me. "Same spot, different season." I didn't want to invest any energy or hope in those four words but they kept playing in my head. I don't know if the Lord felt pity seeing me in that place but His Spirit began to stir things inside me. That same evening, I spoke to my former pastor and just poured out everything I was carrying. It was like an emotional dump. He heard the pain in my voice as I cried through my words of wanting to die. After he listened, he spoke. He ended our call with a prayer. For the first time since I'd been in the pits, I felt hopeful. The feeling of despair wasn't as heavy.

It took two months for me to share this secret with a couple of girlfriends. Others are now finding out because of this book. During this time, I wasn't studying the Word diligently as I had been doing or even referring to it. But there was something else serving as a temporary bridge, Christian music. I found myself flipping between two stations and those songs encouraged me. They ministered to me. They played a role in my renewal.

> *The devil thought he had me, thought that my life was over.*
> *He thought by now I'd give up, he thought I had no more.*
> *But that's when someone greater, stepped in my situation.*
> *My morning now has begun, HE turned it!*
> *—Tye Tribbett*

I can happily say I am no longer in that place where I wanted to end my life. With each day that passes, I conclude that if I'm still here, despite my wish, my past, what the enemy has done and the people he's used to further his goal, it's because God still wants me here because He's not done with me. And if you're reading (or listening to this), He's not done with you either. Remember sis, eyes have not seen... God isn't upset with you for wanting to cut His plan short by ending your life. He hasn't disowned you. He still loves you, and because of His compassion, you and I get to experience His grace in a way that's unbelievable and unaltered.

God wants to transform you into a new person, but it can only be done by changing the way you think. Why? Because thoughts become things. Be it good or bad, the more you think of something or meditate on it, the closer you are to attracting that thing into your life. It's important that you allow God to renew your mind and change your thoughts because that's what will propel you out of the place of darkness and gloom. Maybe a relationship ended on bad terms, the man you loved betrayed you. Maybe you lost that promotion to someone "undeserving." Maybe you didn't get that dream job. Maybe you weren't accepted into that program you'd been hoping for. Maybe you got a prognosis you didn't expect. Maybe your life isn't going the way you desired or envisioned, despite your greatest efforts. God is speaking to you this very moment. That still voice you hear encouraging you, trying to give you new ideas; a different perspective, that's Him. He doesn't want you to quit or give up. Your life is bigger and greater than you.

The enemy is out here pointing people to death's doorway. Can you believe how common it has become for people to take their own lives? He's targeting us one by one because he knows we carry a gift. One that can save; one that will glorify God. Why would he tell Jesus (in His moment of human weakness) to jump off the mountain and quote scripture to support his challenge? He knew the gift that was Jesus Christ. He saw it, recognized it, and didn't want any of us to partake in or enjoy that gift. The enemy understood what Christ's

Day 8

death and resurrection meant for the world. I can tell you this; He also knows what your gift(s) mean to the world.

Notice, you don't often see or hear the devil making these challenges to you when you're in a great place. He feeds off weakness, and depression is his stomping ground. Once he's successfully gotten you to isolate yourself, he goes full force because he knows he's not competing with other voices pouring positivity, hope, and love into you. But here's a reminder, greater is He that lives *in* you!

Trust the Holy Spirit. He will never ask or tell you to end God's plan prematurely. That is never the voice of God.

Additional Scriptures

Romans 8:35
Ecclesiastes 7:17
Luke 4:9

Prayer

Dear God, thank you for not giving up on me, even when I gave up on myself. Thank you for the angels you sent to uplift me and for your Holy Spirit's determination to keep speaking to me. I know you've already forgiven me but I want to ask you anyway. I'm sorry for resting in the place of darkness. Forgive me for those emotions. I know you love me. I believe in my heart that you do and that you want what's best for me because you're a good Father. I ask you today to help me to identify this dark place when it appears on the horizon and help me to turn away from it quickly. When I am unable to do it on my own, support me with your Holy Spirit and give me the energy to run away from it and into your arms. I ask that you give me opportunities to share my experience with other believers as a form of encouragement because it's always hard when we think we're going through something alone. I'm grateful that the devil didn't win this battle and even more grateful that your plan for me is not yet completed. May I continue to seek you and receive a daily renewal from you in my mind. In Jesus' name I pray, Amen.

Reflection of the Day: Are you allowing the pressures of the world, family, or self-imposed goals to weigh you down and to keep you down?

You may think that Christ's love for you has disappeared but it hasn't. He has not abandoned you and certainly has not distanced His love for you. It may be difficult to reconcile this if your thoughts are still being controlled by the enemy. That's why the Lord wants to change your thinking and renew your mind, daily.

*If you or someone you know needs help, please don't be afraid to ask. See below for resources.

SAMHSA Treatment Referral Hotline: 1-877-662-HELP (4357)

National Alliance on Mental Health Helpline: 1-800-950-NAMI (6264)

_____

_____

_____

_____

Day 8

Sister to Sister

Day 9
Self-Control

~Key Scripture~

Romans 8:12 📖 Therefore, dear brothers and sisters, you have no obligation to do what your sinful nature urges you to do.

~Discussion~

How easy is it to give into temptation? How many times have you conceded on a decision to do something that you felt contrary about? Your favorite store is having a sale and you have enough money to treat yourself but you also know that you have a savings goal. Since we're in the YOLO (you only live once) era, you decide to treat yourself because that savings goal isn't going anywhere but the sale and your items will. If you struggle with spending or are a "shopaholic," then this "sale" could've been a test.

The issue of temptation reveals an underlying character trait (Fruit of the Spirit) that many of us struggle with, self-control.

Imagine being told you can't succeed because you lack self-control. Your lack of self-control is seen directly through your response to temptation. We know a couple of things about self-control. Having it is a gift. We also know people who exercise self-control also have the ability to overcome temptation.

A lot of times when you hear people discussing temptation, it typically involves fornication or infidelity. While that is a real area of struggle for some, it is not the only form of temptation.

What is temptation? Why is it bad? Why do we instinctively know that the temptation itself is not good for us? When I think about temptation, I associate it with unjustified desires that always have consequences, even if I don't see them immediately.

If you're a dessert kind of a girl who also values her health, having daily desserts may not be a justified desire. And the reality is, you're not going to wake up three days after eating cheesecake with an extra roll on your stomach. But, if you keep with it and don't maintain an active exercise routine, you will eventually see that roll—plus some, the consequence. So is having a slice of cheesecake justified, when you know you don't workout or that it's against your diet, maybe. But we know what's NOT justified and that's having a slice three nights in a row and then wondering by the end of the week, why or how you gained five additional pounds.

I think for some believers, we think it's "cute" in a sense to blame God when we fail or fall weak to our temptation. We say, "Well, God knows everything; He knows I'm weak, so why tempt me with _____." Let me share a secret with you. God does not tempt. So, whatever temptation you may have faced, was not spearheaded by Him. It's not in His nature. It's not His character. God is not out to get you. God loves you and wants you to succeed and thrive. He's not planning tricks to trip you up. But I know one who is... the enemy. The living God is Holy. He is righteous, too righteous to get involved in the tempting of people just to show them their weaknesses or inadequacies. Instead, He loves us enough to cover our shame and condemnation from the world.

Remember James 1:13 tells us God does not tempt. Also, beware, Jesus was tempted by the enemy and Luke 4:13 tells us that the enemy will try again.

∼Additional Scriptures∼

Romans 6:12
James 1:14
1 Corinthians 10:13
Luke 22:40
Galatians 5:16

∼Prayer∼

Dear God, I thank you because you are never-changing and because of that, I can rest in confidence knowing that the temptations I encounter aren't from you. I'm also thankful because despite the end result of my temptation, your love for me doesn't wane or waiver. While I am grateful for your unconditional love, my love for you moves me to live righteously but I know that I cannot do that on my own. I need you. I ask that as temptations come my way, or I willingly expose myself to them, that your Holy Spirit will strengthen me, convict me with a burning desire to choose the way of escape that you've prepared for me. Make that escape clear to me. I thank you in advance for doing this and more, thank you for growing me in self-control. In Jesus' name, Amen.

Reflection of the Day: Temptations will come but so will your exit; you just have to say no.

_____

_____

_____

Sister to Sister

Day 10
Goal-Digger

∼Key Scripture∼

Ecclesiastes 11:6 📖 Plant your seed in the morning and keep busy all afternoon, for you don't know if profit will come from one activity or another—or maybe both.

∼Discussion∼

Being a goal-digger requires action, just like being a believer. While God can bless whatever He wants; whenever He wants; however, He wants, it's reasonable to say, He's not blessing ideas, but rather the action and activity behind them. Remember earlier when we discussed faith and how it requires action? Right, same thing with having goals—they too, require activity on your part. In the parable Jesus shares with His disciples in Matthew 25:21, Jesus doesn't say, 'Well thought' or 'well-planned' my good and faithful servant. He says, "Well done." So, what are *you* doing?

What's that thing you always wanted to do but got busy and let it go? You know what it is; it lingers in the back of your mind. What's that dream you had before the dream killers and dream snatchers got in your head? If you knew the date and time of your sunset, what's the one goal you would work fervently at accomplishing? For me, it's this devotional. I'm not a minister by education or training but I believe that we all have the ability to minister, according to the gifts God has given us. I always knew I'd write something and as a matter of fact, a few years before this devotional came to be, I started a novel. I never completed it though; it wasn't my passion. When I rededicated my life to Christ a few years later, I saw a void, which became an opportunity. I hadn't come across a devotional that spoke to women in my demographic the way we're speaking. I found myself saying, someone should write a devotional for Black women, professional women of color who are trying to maintain their integrity; live righteous; and have morals in a world where none of this is popular or widely accepted anymore. While I was saying that, the Holy Spirit responded clearly to me, "Then why don't you write it?" I replied, "Because I ain't no preacher or minister; I don't have the credentials to do that; and who's gonna read it?!" So He replied to me and simply said, "You've heard, if you build it, they will come. Well, if you write it, they will read." That stuck with me! And that, friend is how this devotional came to be.

Now, I'm sure this dialogue isn't unique to me. You've probably experienced something similar or are currently having this conversation. Is this a sign?

What gifts do you have? What do people say you're good at? What do you find yourself doing naturally, with ease and pleasure? Have you ever stopped to think about these things? You realize that's God, right? Philippians 2:13 tells us that God is working in us, giving us the desire and the power to do what pleases Him. Sis, you *already* have it in you. So what are you waiting on?

Are you waiting on someone else to see your gifts and abilities and tap into them for you? Because believe me, that can happen, and the gift that you didn't care to grow will be nurtured by others through you, for their benefit. Are you

DAY 10

waiting on someone else to invest in you? Why not invest in yourself? If God gave you this idea, equipped you with the gift, talent, and ability to bring it to fruition, why do you need someone else to do the initial work? No one should ever have more skin in the game for what God assigned to you than you.

Listen, there are times when we see what we have but don't make the time to understand it, mold it, or even try to use it, because we're preoccupied with fillers. Fillers; things—usually invaluable in the grand scheme of things—that distract us from meaningful activities or pursuits. How many times have you been given the opportunity to try something new that's been on your radar for a while but you couldn't because the timing was bad? You were already working on something. How many times have you shied away from an opportunity because you were afraid of what you would or would not produce? Will you strike gold the first time you go digging? Probably not. But if you keep digging, you will. If you have presented God's idea back to Him, after asking for His guidance along the way; done your research and prepared; if you have done *your* part, do you think God will not show up and do His? Where's your faith, boo? Do you think God gave you gifts, talents, and abilities; inspired you to use them to create something that will glorify Him, only for you to turn around and say, "Nah, this isn't for me. I can't... or I don't...?" Seriously? This isn't the time to delay your surrender to His calling. Imagine the lives you could be improving; the world you could be changing; the blessing you could be if you would simply go for it.

Is it a business? Is it a prayer group? Is it a charitable act? Is it a new or different career path? Is it a podcast? What is it? You may not think it's important enough. Perhaps the timing isn't right—if only we knew how much time we actually had, huh?

Sister to Sister

I'm reminded of the story Jesus shares about the master and his three servants in Matthew 25:14.

You may not think you're good enough. Can I tell you something? I've heard pastors say, "God doesn't always call the qualified, but He always qualifies the called."

Remember as a believer, wherever you go, wherever you are, you are the Lord's representative. There are nonbelievers who have not and may not ever step foot inside a physical church. But you friend, *are* the church. You could very well be the first and only encounter a nonbeliever makes with Christ. Wouldn't it be a wonder to see that encounter occur through your fulfillment of your God-given goal?

Additional Scriptures

Proverbs 16:3
Proverbs 14:23
Proverbs 31:18
Proverbs 6:9-11
Colossians 3:23

Prayer

Dear God, thank you for dreams, visions, creativity, skills, talents, abilities, gifts, and all the good things you give me so generously. Thank you for placing your desire in my heart and for trusting me with that gift—that I would use it for your glory. Please forgive me for the times where I took you for granted by discounting or diminishing what you gave me. Forgive me for comparing myself and what I have or don't have to others. Forgive me for the times when I stopped gazing at you and gave my attention to the fillers. I am grateful to know that you haven't given up on me despite my giving up

Day 10

on myself. I'm even more grateful to know that because of your unfailing love for me, you will never give up on me. Today, I rededicate myself to you. I say, "Yes to your will, your vision, and plan for my life." Give me a refreshing blow within me that renews not only my hope in you but my desires. I want to hear you say, "Well done" to me. I want your approval and I want my life to glorify you. So, here I am, open, available, and with a willing heart. Help me figure this out and connect me with the right person(s) to see this through. Whenever I begin to doubt this, I ask that you cause your Holy Spirit to speak a word of encouragement to me and snap me out of that place. I'm nervous and excited. I'm anxious and contemplative. But most of all, I am trusting you. In Jesus' name, Amen.

Reflection of the Day: If God gave you the idea, don't abandon it when challenges arise; it's all a part of God's plan. Remember Proverbs 16:4.

_____

_____

_____

_____

_____

_____

_____

_____

Sister to Sister

Day 11
Fearlessness

⁓**Key Scripture**⁓

Isaiah 41:10 📖 Don't be afraid, for I am with you. Don't be discouraged, for I am your God. I will strengthen you and help you. I will hold you up with my victorious right hand.

⁓**Discussion**⁓

God has not given you or me a spirit of fear. That's 2 Timothy 1:7. I stop here at this point in the verse because of a word many of us often casually read past without fully appreciating. Spirit. The word 'spirit' is significant because in Ephesians 6:12, we are told that we are not wrestling against flesh and blood or people for that matter (though it may appear that way) but against spirits and principalities.

It's also important to recognize the intentional rejection of what we may have willingly (unknowingly) accepted as our reality versus what God actually intended. As we continue to read 2 Timothy 1:7, it goes on to tell us that while we are not given a spirit of fear or timidity, we are given one of power, love, and self-discipline. Whew! That last part is so deep and could be a sermon in and of itself but that's not our focus right now.

So I am restating my first question. What are you afraid of or for? Take a moment and write down your fears, every single one. Yes, that one too. This is *your* truth moment. The only way we can cancel your fear(s) is by acknowledging them and then seeing what our heavenly Father says about each one.

Sometimes, saying what your fear is, can stir something within you; that something being the Holy Spirit, to give you our Father's reality check instead of the world's view.

Now that you've written down your fears, ask yourself, why are you afraid? I once had a fear that I would not fulfill my heart's desire to actually practice law or pay off my student loan debt. I graduated from law school at the most inopportune time, during the financial crisis and recession. I didn't have a job secured and was studying for the bar exam.

Though it implicitly exists, God didn't *give* me a spirit of fear. I took it. Though it is intangible, I made it tangible when I assigned that spirit to a specific thing.

Several years ago, I lost a meaningful relationship and friendship. When it ended, I felt alone and incapable of being loved. I feared that I would never know what it was to be loved by a man God designed for me. As a matter of fact, I feared that God hadn't designed a man for me. Through my tears, I cried out to God, "Who will take the time to get to know me—all of me?" This was a decade-long friendship. He was the only man to know me as well as he did and *that* didn't come easy for either of us. I feared that because of my complexities and invisible wall, no other man would invest his time or energy in getting to know me. No other man would love me the way I loved and deserved to be loved. But then our heavenly Father reminded me of some things. It took a while to accept His word because when you allow fear to grab a hold of your mind *and* heart, it's almost impossible to separate it from the truth.

DAY 11

I feared that I wasn't good enough to be loved when the truth is; I was accepting pieces, fragments of love, trying to create a whole heart when God had already given me His. He gave me Jesus for free, with no expectation that I'd return the love.

I feared my complexities would run future suitors away but then Psalms 139:14 (KIV) reminded me that I am "fearfully and wonderfully made." Another Bible translation says, "Thank you for making me so wonderfully complex!"

I had to start confessing what the Word of God says over my life and not that spirit of fear, which had taken up full residency in my mind.

As I write this today, September 6, 2018, I am still single but much happier and better. I am content with God and my heart is full with satisfaction. I know that He desires for me to be with the right man and if I'm being honest, that lost "situationship" was a fail and I knew it. I actually predicted its ending, a year before it happened. We weren't equally yoked. He was not God's best for me. He wasn't going to challenge me to be a better servant or believer; he barely believed in the Lord himself! But it didn't soften the hurt or lessen the pain of betrayal I felt when things came to an end and my eyes were opened to the revelations that followed.

I promised myself I would wait on God because the next man will be my husband. No pressure: it simply means, I know who I am and whose I am. I know my worth and what I have to offer. I don't have to waste my time with fillers and don't think it's fair to waste their time either.

So how do you address your fears? Well, that's going to take some investment of your time. Here are three ways to confront your fears.

1) Search the Bible and read the text in its context.

2) Meditate on the opposite of that fear.

3) Be honest with yourself and with God. Make no mistake, God is not mocked. He already knows the truth, your heart, and your thoughts.

As a believer, there will come a time when you will be challenged simply because you are a believer or because of your faith in God. It can come in the form of a compromise, or arrangement that seems necessary as the only or best way to get what you want or deserve. You may feel excluded, disliked or ignored. It can even come in a passive-aggressive form. If that's you, right now, remember God's word in Isaiah 51:7, which says, "… Do not be afraid of people's scorn nor fear their insults." The reason you have nothing to fear is because of what our heavenly Father told us earlier in Isaiah 41:10.

Additional Scriptures

Psalms 56:3
Joshua 1:9
Deuteronomy 31:6
Romans 8:15
Proverbs 29:25
John 14:27

Prayer

Dear God, I love you. Please forgive me for giving fear a place in my heart and in my mind, when you didn't give it to me or design me to dwell in it. Thank you for your son, my Savior, Jesus Christ who is a constant reminder of your unfailing love for me. Thank you for making me complex and for being

Day 11

patient and understanding of me, your creation. Now God, I declare as of today, this moment, whatever fear(s) that has (or have) been plaguing my being and blocking your blessings in my life, be bound up and cast into the pit of hell along with all the other spirits that are contrary to your Word and will for my life. I declare that where there was fear, it has been replaced with your peace and blessed assurance in Jesus' name. I declare this and thank you for already doing it, in Jesus' name, Amen.

Reflection of the Day: What if you trusted God more than your fear(s)?

_____

_____

_____

_____

_____

_____

_____

_____

_____

_____

_____

_____

_____

Sister to Sister

Day 12
Positively Thinking

~Key Scripture~

Proverbs 4:23 📖 Guard your heart above all else, for it determines the course of your life.

~Discussion~

How fast do you to go from 0 to 100 when thinking about how something went wrong? I'll be honest with you; it can take me under 30 seconds to allow thoughts of doubt and concern to turn into a full-fledged worry fest. It's as if my mind is already preconditioned to think the worst just because of a hiccup. It also doesn't help that my mother is a worry wart. I think she may have inadvertently instilled that bad habit in me.

Growing up, I never knew there was a correlation between negative thinking and negative results. Yes, the Bible says, "… As a man thinks in his heart, so is he …," but I didn't understand what that meant.

In Philippians 4:8, Paul tells us what to think about; things that are true, and honorable and right and pure and lovely and admirable. We are told to think about things that are excellent and worthy of praise. Why? Because it pleases God.

It requires little effort for us to fear the worst and dwell on negative thoughts. But when you do that, you're actually opening a door for the enemy to walk right into your life and wreak havoc. Sis, did you forget that God knows all and sees all? That's a thought that should encourage you even in your lowest of lows. Let me tell you why. Jeremiah 29:11 tells us, God knows the plans He has for us. Plans... plural. So there isn't just one use for you, He has multiple uses for you and what may seem like a failure in the flesh is a win in the spirit! Why do I say that? Well, for starters, God gives us free will. This means He isn't forcing Himself on us. He wants us to intentionally choose to serve Him and love Him. Now, although He gives us free will, He already knows what our decisions will be every single time before we even make them; both the good ones and bad ones. Knowing this, He's given us a foolproof ending, meaning, no matter what our decision is along the journey, there's already a "recalculating" taking place to get you to His desired destination, a fulfillment of His purpose, *see* Romans 8:28.

Now for some, it may work in your life because His plans for good are to give you a future and a hope. This is your win. Whether or not you make mistakes, they've all been accounted for and the end is still a victory. Let *that* sink in. So, if the "game" is rigged in your favor—be it on the job dealing with a coworker or boss, at home with your family, in your marriage, or relationships (romantic and platonic), that means all the negative thoughts you allow to dwell does nothing to help you. Rather, you develop negative energy and naturally project that onto others. And if they are not saved or mature in their faith, they'll return that same negative energy that stemmed from your negative thoughts back to you, therefore perpetuating the negativity that is attacking you. Yikes!

If you haven't already heard this, thoughts can become things. Whatever you meditate on or think about a lot can and will happen, be it good or bad. But listen, you control that because you control your thoughts. And that starts with your heart. I believe Paul knew this and that's why he clearly told us what to spend our time thinking about.

So how do we change our thoughts from negative to positive? Ephesians 4:23 tells us to let the Holy Spirit renew our thoughts and attitudes. We must intentionally choose to fix our thoughts on God because it shows Him that we trust in Him because He promises to keep us in perfect peace.

In Romans 12:2, we are told to be transformed by the renewing of our mind. Our mind is powerful. The thoughts we think are powerful. This is why we have to actively fight against those easy to think negative thoughts. Don't accept them. Don't allow them to become your reality.

Additional Scriptures

Romans 12:2
1 Peter 5:8-9
Psalms 139:23
Isaiah 26:3
2 Corinthians 10:5
Psalms 104:34

Prayer

Dear God, thank you for thinking of me. When I think of how you love me and demonstrate your love for me, daily, I am ashamed of how I allow negative thoughts to intrude on who I know you to be. Please forgive me for providing those bad and unrighteous thoughts a home in my mind. I understand that these thoughts don't just come out from anywhere but rather they are reflections of what's in my heart. So, I ask you to purify my heart. Remove those negative traits and feelings that are within me and replace them with your traits. Fill my heart with righteousness so that my thoughts will be righteous. Create in me a clean heart, Lord, and renew a loyal spirit within me. And Father, when the enemy tries to take me back to those old familiar places, I declare in the mighty name of Jesus that your Holy Spirit will rise up in its authority causing me to capture those thoughts, cast them out, and immediately replace them with your truth. May my thoughts from here on out glorify you and reflect your Lordship over my life. In Jesus' name I pray, Amen.

Reflection of the Day: Your thoughts will either lead you to your destiny or keep you from it.

_____

_____

_____

_____

_____

_____

_____

_____

_____

DAY 12

Sister to Sister

Day 13
Don't Stay Mad

~Key Scripture~

Psalms 37:8 📖 Stop being angry! Turn from your rage! Don't lose your temper—it only leads to harm.

~Discussion~

Why are you so mad? You've heard the question before, "Who hurt you?" Why do so many things upset you? Why are you so easily triggered? Why can't you release that anger?

James 1:20 tells us that human anger does not produce the righteousness God desires. So we know, our anger isn't pleasing to God.

There are many things both within our control and outside of our control that can lead us down an angry path. I'll confess, I used to take myself way too seriously, and consequently, was in a constant state of anger; but I internalized my anger. As I changed my perspective on things, and accepted how God was never surprised by my life's events, I began to release some of that anger. But please know, it did not happen overnight. In reading and studying the Word, I began to appreciate Ephesians 6:12 and the spiritual warfare that's taking place in the supernatural. Meaning, I came to realize that it's not always about me. Yeah, I may not like the way someone spoke to me or how they handled a situation, but it also may not be them, it could be a force using them to attack me and throw me off track. Perhaps that person is having a bad day. Maybe they are just grumpy. What I know is that as soon as I decided to consciously give grace and reject the negative energy directed toward me, I began to experience God's peace.

Oftentimes, it's the disappointment I feel from the unfulfilled expectations; when I've been intentionally misrepresented, misunderstood, or deceived. We all know what anger feels like—blood boiling, internal conflict with no peace regarding what to do, or how to reciprocate that feeling and avenge yourself. The thoughts that begin to emerge as a result of my anger can be dangerous.

Not only are those thoughts dangerous, but so are the words we speak out of anger. Those words, once they leave our mouths can never be returned or forgotten.

God doesn't want us to be angry and He tells us to get rid of it in Ephesians 4:31. Even when we have every reason to be angry, He doesn't want that for us, and if we must be angry, it shouldn't be a constant behavior. James 1:19 tells us we must be slow to get angry. Can you imagine if God got as angry as we did, as quickly as we did? Yeah, that's pretty scary. As believers, we shouldn't be triggered by everything; that's part of our spiritual discipline. When we are easily angered, it shows our lack of spiritual maturity because we immediately consume or allow ourselves to become consumed by the anger. Sometimes completely failing to realize that the event that led to our "natural" feeling of anger (or angry reaction)—though it may have been "carried" out by a person—was the device of the enemy. Because remember what I said earlier, we are not fighting against mere humans, but against evil rulers, authorities, and spirits of the unseen world.

So yes, while this person may have done or said something egregious and unforgivable, unfortunately, they may have simply been a pawn in the enemy's evil game of spiritual warfare against you. Unlike God, the enemy isn't omnipresent, so he has to use people to get to you and attack you, and trust me, they are on standby. The enemy wants an angry reaction from you because that's his window of opportunity to get you to sin. It makes him look good, and you—much easier to use, easier to be manipulated, and easier to abuse.

I believe that's why Paul tells us in Ephesians 4:27 that anger gives a foothold to the devil. We often hear people say the preceding verse, which says, "Don't let the sun go down while you are still angry." But the why is found in verse 27.

So, how do we resolve our anger issues? By asking God for His help. But know this, once you do this, know you will be faced with more challenges ahead. However, this time you'll be better prepared because you will also be more aware of your response and reactions. The Holy Spirit will convict you and give you God's peace.

ꙮAdditional Scripturesꙮ

Psalms 4:4
Proverbs 19:11
Ephesians 4:2
Matthew 5:22
Proverbs 14:29
Ecclesiastes 7:9
Romans 12:19

 Prayer

Dear God, please forgive me for how I've acted. It's no secret to you how I've responded to others and situations. Looking back at that version of myself disappoints me. I want to reflect your presence in all areas of my life. I know what I'm asking for means that some tests will be sent my way, but I believe that by the power of your Holy Spirit, I have the ability to pass them. However, if I fail, I'm grateful to know that you won't turn away from me, but rather because of your patient love for me, you'll simply continue to test me until I pass. Make me more aware of those things that I allow to trigger me. Grow me to the point where I am not easily moved by actions, inactions, disappointments, lies, or other things that would normally get a reaction out of me. I want to get so lost in your Word that people around me see the change you've made in my life. That way, they too can seek you and discover your truth, which brings peace. Thank you for not getting angry with me as I tend to do with others. I can't handle your fury. Thank you for defending me and for avenging me. May I continue to show you my dependence on you by letting you show up for me and letting your light shine through me, in Jesus' name I pray, Amen.

Reflection of the Day: One of the best out-of-body experiences you can have is seeing yourself not respond or react the way you used to. #Growth

_____

_____

_____

Day 13

Sister to Sister

Day 14
More Grace

~Key Scripture~

Matthew 18:23-27 📖 The Kingdom of Heaven can be compared to a king who decided to bring his accounts up to date with servants who had borrowed money from him. In the process, one of his debtors was brought in who owed him millions of dollars. He couldn't pay, so his master ordered that he be sold—along with his wife, his children, and everything he owned—to pay the debt. But the man fell down before his master and begged him, 'Please, be patient with me, and I will pay it all.' Then his master was filled with pity for him, and he released him and forgave his debt.

~Discussion~

This story is often told in the context of forgiveness but when I asked the Holy Spirit for a story that demonstrated grace, it came to mind. See, the grace that was demonstrated was the forgiveness of the man's debt. He didn't deserve that; he didn't earn it. From what I can tell, he was in no position to bargain or offer anything of value to settle his debt. The master's decision to forgive this man of his debt was an act of grace. Because we know what the consequence was—the man, his wife, children, and EVERYTHING he owned were to be sold in an effort to repay this debt. Yet, after begging and pleading, he got something he didn't deserve, a cancellation of debt; a clean slate. What makes this story so fascinating is what happens immediately after. We learn that the same man went to a person who owed him money and demanded to be repaid. When *that* person did the same begging and pleading, the man who was the recipient of grace, forgot what that looked like.

Many of us have benefited from grace; that is, getting what you don't deserve. And sometimes, we get it without even asking. Maybe you can think of a time when as a child, you did something that certainly warranted an unforgettable consequence. Then you waited on the punishment, and while waiting for the moment of reckoning, your parent looked at you and said, "I'm going to let this slide." You're naturally grateful but also nervous because you're in disbelief about what should've been, that was not. You almost walked on eggshells because you didn't want that pardon to backfire, and subconsciously, you just knew with certainty that you were going to get in trouble and the punishment was just being delayed. Later on you learn that sometimes, the decision to not punish *was* the lesson. That, my friend is grace.

Or maybe as an adult, you did something you knew would come back to bite you on the behind. You expected to get in trouble; you expected the fallout to be severe. You were even a bit panicked at the thought of how bad the situation was going to be. You anxiously awaited the penalty and were in mental anguish trying to prepare for the repercussions. Then, the other shoe finally dropped; everything hit the fan but, nothing happened. That, girlfriend, was God's grace... and mercy.

Romans 3:23 reminds us that everyone has sinned; we all fall short of God's glorious standard. Yet God, in His grace, freely makes us right in His sight. He did this through Christ Jesus when He freed us from the penalty of our sins.

DAY 14

In case you haven't figured it out, GRACE is a benefit you receive that you do not deserve or have not earned. The best example of grace is God's love. Because we are born sinners; we could never be worthy of God's unfailing love on our own. This is because as sinners, we stand in direct opposition to who He is, HOLY. Though God hates sin, He chose to cover us with His grace so that we could be recipients of His unconditional, unfailing, and unwavering love. He doubles down on His position by declaring that nothing can separate us from His love for us.

We see God's demonstration of grace in our lives through His sacrifice of Jesus and our believing in Him. Look, there's no amount of rule-following that would save us because we're imperfect beings. But believing in the perfect one is what saves us. There is literally nothing we could do, offer, or exchange with God to match His grace. He gave it to us freely. And if we are followers or attempting to be followers, the grace He gives us every single day should be seen in our encounters and interactions with our brothers and sisters.

Why is it important for us to offer grace to everyone? Because we are God's representatives on earth—at our jobs, homes, grocery stores, churches, and even when we're commuting in traffic. Yep! Rush-hour traffic.

Rather than think the worst or expect the worst, maybe give that person the benefit of the doubt. That's grace. Imagine having to make a phone call to handle some business and the customer service representative is not pleasant. That is a frustrating situation to be in because, not only have you been on hold for over 20 minutes, but you've been trying to resolve this issue for a while. Only to end up with someone who doesn't seem to be interested in either doing their job, assisting you, or both. You could easily tap into your flesh and raise your voice, have a bad attitude, and just mirror their rudeness. But as believers in Christ, we're not called to take the easy road or mirror the world. We're expected to tap into the Spirit and let Him guide us so that we reflect God. Grace in this situation is putting your phone on mute, taking a deep breath and telling yourself, "This, right here, isn't about me." That person's negative spirit isn't about you, sis. They don't even know you. Maybe they are having a bad day, week, or month. Maybe they wanted to take off from work that day but simply couldn't afford to? Maybe they lost a loved one. There's a host of maybes we could consider, including maybe they are just nasty people. Even so, grace is reciprocal; meaning, the same undeserved beneficial treatment you receive from God is the same undeserved treatment you should give freely. Remember, we are all flawed human beings. Be more gracious.

Additional Scriptures

Romans 11:6
James 4:6
Acts 15:11

Prayer

Dear God, thank you for showing me grace, more grace than I'm sure I've shown to others. Please forgive me for the times I disappointed you by being selfish and not sharing your grace. I know I don't deserve this generous gift but I'm reminded that if YOU, the creator of all things, who sits high above the heavens could show me grace and deal with me as such, surely, I can show grace to the people I encounter and engage with. Maybe, by my positive response, they'll be curious about you and want to learn about you. Maybe they will be gracious with others. I know I'm not done using or receiving your

DAY 14

grace. So I pray that as often as I am the recipient of your grace, that you'll grant me opportunities to share your grace with others. I thank you in advance for doing this and so much more, in Jesus' name, Amen.

Reflection of the Day: Remember, being gracious to people you already know or like doesn't distinguish you from unbelievers, anyone can do that. Try showing grace to an enemy or a stranger—that's the game changer!

Sister to Sister

Day 15
Less Worry

~Key Scripture~

Matthew 6:27 📖 Can all your worries add a single moment to your life?

~Discussion~

Some of us have become so used to losing that we don't know what it feels like to win. And consequently, we have forgotten how to trust God because we continue to doubt Him.

You want to know a telltale of a pseudo-believer? Watch how he or she responds to an unplanned, unexpected, out-of-their-control event. Many of us *say* we believe in God and His son Jesus but when the time comes to be tested, which allows us the opportunity to demonstrate just how much we believe, we fail; sometimes miserably. Why is that? How does this happen? How can someone who attends church regularly and believe that God is the I AM find themselves in distress, worrying, and full of anxiety about circumstances? What makes this possible? They may not be tethered to the Word like they used to be or need to be, which results in worrying. This isn't to say that we shouldn't think about things happening in our lives; that's not problematic. The problem lies in how we think about the situation and the energy we direct towards it.

Have you ever heard the saying, 'If you're going to pray, then don't worry. And if you're going to worry, then don't pray?' This adage speaks to where and how we choose to focus our energy and our faith. See, if a circumstance that you're unprepared for presents itself in your life, you have two ways of responding. You can either look at it and say, "OK God, this is all you, because I don't have the ability to fix this and get the result I desire; I need a miracle." Or you can look at it and say, "OK God, this is a lot and I don't know how I'm going to resolve it; I need a miracle." I want to point something out between the two declarations. First, just to be clear, BOTH declarations are from believers; however, only one surrenders to God. There's no partial surrendering. You either do or you don't. The first declaration is a surrender and acknowledgment of God's sovereignty and rule over your life. The second declaration is disguised as surrender, but it is not. The moment we say, "I don't know how I'm going to ..." we automatically remove the Lordship title that we claim to give God from Him. As a result, we instantly feel an overwhelming amount of pressure because we know we can't fix it.

You ever see someone you know going through a season or challenging time, yet, their spirit is higher than expected? And when they discuss their situation, they seem to be full of optimism? You may look at them and think, "Oh 'Fake it 'til you make it' or 'They're putting on a good front.'" However, there are those of us who see that and are encouraged because we know that what we're seeing and hearing is a direct reflection of that person's relationship with God. They fall in that "surrender" group and truly mean it when they say, "God, I can't handle this and am not going to act like I can because this is all YOU." So although they are going through real challenges, they are also experiencing a surreal level of peace that can only come from knowing, trusting, and having an

DAY 15

intimate relationship with God. God doesn't want us to live a life filled with worry and anxiety. Sis, He didn't create us for that. That's not part of our job description here on earth. Our worrying does not glorify God. Experiencing anxiety at every turn does not honor Him. Our lives are supposed to reflect God's presence and a critical difference between us, and nonbelievers is the peace we're afforded through our relationship with Him.

Next time you're faced with a challenge, no matter how little or big it is, I want to encourage you to try something different. Perhaps you're dealing with something right now. Well, I'll say this; you've already tried worrying, which always brings its companion anxiety along. Maybe you tried handing it over to God but you weren't fully committed to giving it all to Him because you were driving yourself mad trying to figure it out.

If you need proof that God doesn't want you to worry about whether or not your needs will be met, read Matthew 6:26— Look at the birds. They don't plant or harvest or store food in barns, for your heavenly Father feeds them. And aren't you far more valuable to Him than they are?

If that isn't enough, let me remind you of Philippians 4:6— Don't worry about anything; instead, pray about everything. Tell God what you need and thank Him for all He has done.

The reason you should feel even more at peace after speaking with God about your situation is because of Psalms 139:16— You saw me before I was born. Every day of my life was recorded in your book. Every moment was laid out before a single day had passed. That right there should have you feeling yourself!

I love this scripture and routinely find myself going back to it when I'm faced with something that would make me want to worry. That's because this scripture literally reminds me that my life, every part of it, is like a rerun episode for God. While you will encounter surprises and say, "Gee, I didn't see that coming," God is NEVER surprised and will never say He didn't see something coming because He knows our end from the very beginning. Not the beginning of our life or our birth but the beginning of the world. That last part, "Every moment was laid out before a single day had passed"— EVERY MOMENT?! That means this moment, this very moment. It means when that situation you didn't see coming, comes, He knew it was coming. It's that positive performance review a month ago and your termination of employment two months later. It's that, no one in your family suffers from this disease yet you tested positive for it and you were just diagnosed. It's that, we were supposed to spend the rest of our lives together and he betrayed me. The list could go on but the good news here is that while it may hurt, frighten, expose, embarrass, humiliate, and frustrate, the situation, whatever it is, IS NOT beyond God's reach or repair.

This means that whatever you're facing right now, He saw it coming and also saw you coming out of it. Now, the length of time that it takes to come out varies from person to person, faith to faith. Nevertheless, God is here, He is present, and most importantly, all-knowing. This means, He has the solution. But how can we get it if we're not talking to Him and handing our problems over to Him? When Paul says in Philippians 4:6, "Tell God what you need," he isn't saying to do this because God doesn't know your needs. Matthew 6:26 and Psalms 139:16 make it clear that He knows. The reason we're told to have that conversation with our heavenly Father is because our heavenly Father wants to hear from us directly.

He wants us to come to Him about those things that we can't solve on our own. Those situations that test us, surprise us, and scare us. He wants us to share our hearts with Him. God desires intimacy and you can't get that from occasional conversations here and there. So how will you respond next time something triggers worry or anxiety within you?

Additional Scriptures

Romans 8:28
Ecclesiastes 3:15
Luke 12:11-12

Prayer

To the all-knowing God who is able to exceed my expectations, thank you. Thank you for being a faithful comforter and righteous defender. Please forgive me for the times I've said I trust you, yet my actions proved otherwise. Forgive me for trying to fix things on my own and not seeking your counsel first. I love you and I know you love me. I know you care for me and only want what is best for me. Help me to lean into you deeper when I'm faced with circumstances beyond my control. Remind me of your Word and give me that peace, your great peace that surpasses understanding. I am so grateful that nothing about my life surprises you because you're more than prepared to be whatever it is I need in that moment. Please, don't let me forget that. I ask that you remove all my worries and anxiety and replace them with inexplicable joy. Make me more aware of my thoughts so that by your Spirit, I can capture those negative and worrisome thoughts and cast them out, in the name of Jesus. Replace those thoughts with your Word and positive affirmations. I thank you for doing this and so much more for me. Thank you for giving me an opportunity to draw nearer to you through my circumstance. May my response to the things I can't control, honor you and bring glory to your name. In Jesus' name I pray, Amen.

Reflection of the Day: You will worry less when you believe that no matter what, it is all part of God's plan.

_____

_____

_____

_____

_____

_____

_____

_____

_____

_____

_____

_____

_____

_____

_____

Day 15

Sister to Sister

Day 16
Giving

~Key Scripture~

Proverbs 11:25 📖 The generous will prosper; those who refresh others will themselves be refreshed.

~Discussion~

As a woman, it seems we are predisposed to give, right? I mean, we are nurturers. We want to ensure that those we love are good. But, what about the unkempt stranger that sits next to us on the train and perhaps starts talking to us? What about the coworker that doesn't engage in many conversations? What about the local community facility that asks for mentors? What about when our church asks for volunteers? We give to those we know but what about those we don't know? What are we giving them?

Giving isn't just monetary. You may be the person thinking, "I donate my clothes to shelters." I ask, "When was the last time you went inside the shelter and asked if they needed help receiving those generous donations?" We can always do more. It's possible that your day-to-day life doesn't put you in these places, but there is always a space that's in need, and you might just be the person that's needed.

Jesus tells us in Luke 6:38, "The amount you give will determine the amount you get back." Yes, you've likely heard

Sister to Sister

this scripture used in reference to tithes and offerings but if you read this in your Bible, it doesn't reference tithes and offerings. This statement, which can also be interpreted as a promise, is a general principle. Give and you will receive.

So you say you want, but what are you giving? Here's something to consider about receiving. You may not receive *it* automatically or when *you* think you should. Something else to consider; you shouldn't be giving with the expectation of, being acknowledged, or holding it over the recipient. Even though a person may benefit directly from your generous gift of resources, be it time, money, or talent, the gift, isn't actually for the person. It's for you. When you give, it's a demonstration of your trust in God to continue to supply you with your needs and wants, and to prosper you.

Don't be mediocre when you give. You've seen it before, someone begrudgingly does something and because their act wasn't rooted in love or come from a willing heart, it was almost best they didn't participate or give at all. If it wouldn't please you, what makes you think it would please God? You know what's hurtful? When we give our money, time, skills, or other resource to someone we know, like a family member or friend, and later remind them of what we did or gave or tell others what we did. Not only is it hurtful... it's not of God. Jesus tells us how we should be giving in Matthew 6:2-4. We all have a measure in which we can give that doesn't burden us. If your finances don't allow for generous giving right now, does your time? One is not better than the other; it's the heart and intent that pleases God.

Lastly, be aware of the heart in which you give. Time can be volunteering, supporting, mentoring, listening, compassion, and any other act that requires you to do something with no direct benefit to you. You don't just do good for those you already know or have a relationship with. You are required to do good for your enemies. As for money, Jesus says quite frankly in Luke 6:33 and 34, "And if you lend money only to those who can repay you, why should you get credit?"

If you want to see a change in what you receive, change the way you give. I encourage you not only by my words, but by God's. If you have been giving generously of your time, money, or talent, ask God to reveal what in your life is blocking His Word from bringing its harvest. Just be prepared for the answer you receive because it may not be what you want to hear.

Additional Scriptures

Proverbs 11:24
Deuteronomy 24:19
1 Timothy 6:18
2 Corinthians 9:10-11

Prayer

God, I just want to say thank you for being the example of what generosity looks like. I'll admit I haven't always been as giving as I should or could be. But I don't want that to be my way of living anymore. So, I ask you to give me your heart. Break my heart for what breaks yours. Open my eyes to see the many opportunities in which I can be a blessing to others. I want to be a generous giver and glorify you through my gifts. I know it might be difficult at first, so please start me off at a measure you know I can handle. If I find myself questioning what it is that I have to offer, I ask that you first forgive me for taking your gifts for granted, and then remind me of them. There are times when I simply forget all the ways in which you've blessed me and that's a blessing in and of itself. But I

Sister to Sister

don't want to ever deny you the glory that you deserve through my act of submission. Help me, Lord. As you continue to bless me, allow me to be a blessing to others in Jesus' name, Amen.

Reflection of the Day: Pay it forward today. Bless someone unexpectedly and see how you feel.

_____

_____

_____

_____

_____

_____

_____

_____

_____

_____

_____

_____

_____

_____

_____

Day 16

Sister to Sister

Day 17
Wisdom

∾Key Scripture∾

James 1:5 📖 If you need wisdom, ask our generous God.

∾Discussion∾

There was a time when having wisdom was valuable and desirable. It was an intangible badge of honor and sense of pride we had for others because it was evident, they knew something. Today, wisdom seems hard to come by, even in believers. It seems as if those who are wise are not sharing their wisdom, while fools wander about sharing their perspective to anyone who will listen; thus, giving the perception that *they* are wise.

Webster's Dictionary defines wisdom as: (1) insight—the ability to discern inner qualities and relationships; (2) judgment—good sense; (3) knowledge—accumulated philosophical or scientific learning; (4) a wise attitude, belief or cause of action. Reading these definitions makes it hard to imagine living this life without wisdom. Yet, many of us do and we suffer greatly for it. God wants us to operate in wisdom but in order to do that, we must first 'obtain' it (or at least *know* that we have it).

See, having wisdom and operating in it are two different things. Said differently, just because we have wisdom doesn't mean we don't make foolish decisions. I believe that as women, God gifted us with this unique gift called wisdom, not simply for our personal benefit, but for that of our family. The problem however is that many of us have not attempted to develop our wisdom, and those of us who do, go about it the wrong way. Proverbs 1:7 tells us that the beginning of wisdom is God, which means that in order to have the insight; judgment; knowledge; or wise attitude, we must be in relationship with God.

Sis, are you in relationship with God? Have you asked Him to develop your gift? It's not too late to get on the right track. You have wisdom within you, and friend, the glow-up that comes with wisdom is something you want to have. Proverbs 9:11 tells us that wisdom will multiply your days and add years to your life! What else do you know offers that outcome? You might wonder, "Well, how *will* wisdom do that?" Easy. By aligning you with God so that you're making the right choices for your life.

Is operating in wisdom that important? YES! Do you understand how valuable having wisdom and operating in it is? Ecclesiastes 7:12 tells us, while "Wisdom and money can get you almost anything, only wisdom can save your life." So again, I ask, "Are you in relationship with God? Have you asked Him to develop your gift?"

You ever watch someone make a tough decision and listen to their reasoning? Listening to their thought process can be revealing as it exposes many things. If you have a relationship with God, He will reveal to you whether or not that person is also led by Him. Wisdom is best seen in the decisions we make. Can I tell you something? When you decide to listen to a person's reasoning, it indicates that you have wisdom.

Day 17

I get it, operating in wisdom doesn't appear to produce short-term benefits and in a time when results are needed yesterday, that's a challenging ask. But might I suggest you consider the long-term gains you make when operating in wisdom. Your reputation will precede you in a positive way. It will defend you, even when you're not around.

Knowing all of this, why isn't everyone dealing in wisdom? Well, simple, because it's hard. Abiding in wisdom requires discipline and that discipline comes with having a consistent relationship with God. Yes, He gives wisdom generously but it's also dependent on our faith in Him. Meaning, we can't ask God for wisdom while also having another source in mind or an alternative. It doesn't work that way with God. He wants us to abide in Him and when we do that, we move in wisdom. This not only sets us apart from the world, but it also glorifies God. However, God isn't about to share the credit for how we operate and the favorable dealings we experience as a result of our wise decisions with anything or anyone. Trust me, you want God's wisdom!

So, why discuss wisdom now, something so passé? Simple. Our lack of it is causing many of us to make decisions that are not beneficial to us in the present or the future. Listen friend, the decisions and life choices we make today will impact our future descendants; just as our ancestors' decisions impacted us. Unfortunately, these days, we hear more about people acting foolish and making foolish decisions than being wise. And no, you don't have to be of a particular age to be wise. You don't even have to have full-circle life events or experiences. Wisdom isn't reserved for those people, but you would think it is because *they* are the ones who seem to have obtained it. King Solomon was relatively young when he became king of Israel. He asked God for wisdom and God gave it to him. He wasn't an elder; he hadn't "lived" life yet.

Regrettably, it seems that we believe or think one must be foolish first, before becoming wise, and that's not true. It doesn't have to be true for you. I'd say the reason we have conditioned ourselves to think that wisdom comes with age is because most of the wise people we come across (or see on television) are older. But that doesn't mean that is God's plan for you. I wonder if we believe wisdom comes with age because society enables us to be fools, making foolish decisions in our youth. Then as we grow older, the expectation that we 'know better' by recognizing our recurring habits, flaws, and mistakes becomes a glaring sense of judgment. Can I share something with you? As long as you are alive, you are not too young or too old to activate wisdom. All you have to do is commit to receiving and exercising it.

Additional Scriptures

Proverbs 14:1
Proverbs 2:6
Proverbs 8:11
Proverbs 14:33
Proverbs 12:15

Prayer

Dear God, I want to be wise. Yes, I want to have your understanding, guidance, and direction in how I move about in this world. Help me to make better decisions by seeking your counsel first. Forgive me for the times that I looked to myself or others for what you desire to share with me. I ask that from this moment forward, you be the influence in my life. Let my life reflect your presence. Let my decisions reflect my relationship with you. And Lord, don't let me take your wisdom for granted by engaging with fools. In Jesus' name I pray, Amen.

DAY 17

Reflection of the Day: You will never look foolish when acquiring wisdom from the Lord.

Sister to Sister

Day 18
My Body is a Temple

～Key Scripture～

1 Corinthians 6:18 📖 Run from sexual sin! No other sin so clearly affects the body as this one does.

～Discussion～

They say sex has a way of clouding your judgment, and if you're aware of that vulnerable moment, you can get your partner to do almost anything you want. That's a strong level of hypnosis and I believe it is part of the reason why God tells us to deprive ourselves from the power of sexual immorality, impurity, and lust.

So, what is fornication? To put it plainly, it is all sexual activity outside of marriage. Even if you don't care about your body, there's someone who does, the Lord. Why? Well, because our bodies were made for Him. Not in a sexual way, but in a holy way. We're told in the key scripture that "no other sin" affects our body like that of fornication. That's because fornication is a direct sin against our own bodies.

Here's what I know to be true for myself. Every time I became intimate with a man, I ALWAYS heard a voice telling me not to do it. Sometimes the voice was loud and annoying in my head, other times it was gentle, yet vigilant. It doesn't matter how aroused I was, how hot and heavy I felt in the moment, that voice always spoke clearly to me. Then it would ask the "what ifs" like, what if you get pregnant, what if he has a disease, what if he isn't the one? Girl, you know this is wrong, he ain't the one. God is here and He's watching you! Honey, the last one always left me shook because the reality was, God *was* there. He's everywhere.

There were many times I'd try (unsuccessfully) to drown out the noise—that voice—by creating my own fantasies. If music were playing, I'd let my mind drift. But there were also times where I believe my heavenly Father saw my determination to ignore Him and satisfy my flesh so He'd turnaround and speak through the guy. Yes, it has happened. Somehow, the guy would stop and ask me questions like, "Are you sure? Are you ready? Do you really want to?" I once had a guy turn me down and, in that moment, I felt rejected. I didn't realize it until much later that the Holy Spirit intervened by speaking to Him and he was obedient... even though I wasn't trying to be.

Sis, you may not be a virgin and that's OK! God doesn't hate you; He isn't ashamed to claim you, and He certainly isn't punishing you because you aren't. We already know that He doesn't have any favorites. You are no different than someone who is and it's not too late to choose celibacy. We are all still sinners and have likely fornicated. It took me realizing that every time I allowed my body to be touched or was intimate with a man who is NOT my husband, I was disappointing God and hurting my physical and spiritual self.

I stopped fornicating for myself and because I love God. Every time I choose not to go over to a man's house knowing what his intentions are, or even having a suspicion as to what they are, every time I decide against letting a man come over who I'm attracted to or have little to no self-control with, every time I stop watching-reading-listening to things that arouse me and get me thinking lustful and sexual thoughts, every time I stop myself from getting intimate with a man or choose not to put myself in a tempting situation, I am showing God that I trust Him. I trust that the man He designed just for me (because all we need is one) exists and I am going to wait.

Friend, I need you to know this, you're not any less saved for fornicating. However, if you don't have a sincere desire to stop, your faith and trust in God might need some more work. You're not alone. Stop letting society tell you who you should be or what you should be doing. Society isn't answering for your decisions on earth or in heaven, you are. Society isn't tucking you in at night either, God is. Remember that. Even when you intentionally disobey Him by choosing yourself (i.e., your flesh), God continues to choose you every day in hopes that you will choose Him too. All He wants you to do is trust Him.

Additional Scriptures

1 Corinthians 6:12
Colossians 3:5
1 Peter 1:17
1 John 4:4

Prayer

Dear God, only you truly know the road that I've traveled to get to where I am and all the life experiences that have made me who I am today. I can't help but be honest with you because you know my heart, my thoughts, and what I'm going to say before I say it. So the truth is, I like feeling desired, being touched, and held. The problem is, sometimes I allow these feelings that my body has, to dominate your Spirit, which also occupies my body. It's not right and it shouldn't be like that, but I get weak. Please, forgive me of my weaknesses. Forgive me for grieving your Holy Spirit. Forgive me for not taking proper care of my body, which is your vessel. When I am broken, you somehow manage to piece me back together and use me. I ask that you'll do that for me today. Help me to turn away from those things that lead me to sin. For the men in my life that I entertain against your will, I ask that you remove them without controversy. Allow me to lose interest in them while being so preoccupied with what glorifies you, that I no longer desire them. I believe you know who and what is best for me. Strengthen my faith in you so that I am as loyal to you as you are to me. I ask all these things in the name of your son, Jesus, and thank you for this better version of me. I like her already. In Jesus' name, Amen.

Reflection of the Day: What's today? Clean slate day! Now act like it.

_____

_____

_____

_____

_____

_____

_____

DAY 18

Sister to Sister

Day 19
It Might Be a Test

~Key Scripture~

Ecclesiastes 3:11 📖 Yet God has made everything beautiful for its own time. He has planted eternity in the human heart, but even so, people cannot see the whole scope of God's work from beginning to end.

~Discussion~

You ever want something so bad you were willing to do anything to get it? Of course you have, who hasn't? There are some things we want that are inspired by God and others that are not. Did you know that there are two sources at play in our lives? Those fundamental sources are good versus evil. It sounds strange and even a bit unnerving or dramatic to hear the word evil associated with you, right? Just about as much as you probably feel convicted or conflicted when you hear the word: sin. Well, the reality is, evil exists and its product or end result (manifestation) is sin; just as good exists and its product or manifestation is righteousness. I know the subject matter today is about patience, but I think a little foundation here might help with understanding why patience is an important character trait that we all must have and exercise regularly. See, when we understand that the two sources in the world inspire our desires then we can grow to appreciate and recognize the difference between the two desires.

So let's go back to our source of inspiration. Just to be clear, although we know at times when our motivation is ill driven, it is important to acknowledge what that could look like. For starters, God does not always assign easy, quick-fix desires. Occasionally, we might get a simple idea but even that tends to develop into something greater because the God we serve is great! But, if you desire something inspired by envy or jealousy, that is not a God-given inspiration or desire. If you want something because someone else, particularly someone you do not like has it, that's not God, sis. Essentially, what I'm saying is if your desire for anything is rooted in showing off (this could be flaunting yourself or any possessions), gaining the approval of others, or attempting to diminish or discredit someone else, it is not God-inspired or God-given.

It is important that we speak truth to this because many of us are aware of it but deny ourselves and others the truth as if God doesn't already know what's in our hearts. If the root of your desire is based on what I just shared, you can't reasonably be upset with God for not giving it to you or hold Him to a promise He didn't even make to you. If God did not place that desire in your heart, you cannot turn around and tell Him that He said He'd give you the desires of your heart. It doesn't work like that friend. God will fulfill the desires He's placed in your heart and He will guide you along the path to achieve them, but you have to put in the work; sometimes it's a little and at other times, it's a lot.

As a result of those evil desires (because if it's not from God, we know it's bad), we find ourselves committing sins so that WE can produce something that God did not promise us, or even worse, manifest something sooner than God promised. By now, you are asking if God did not approve of, or if He knew it wasn't for you, why did He let you get it or allow it to happen? Well, that's a deeper conversation to have at another

Day 19

time. But, the takeaway here is the lesson on patience. Because even when our intentions are shady rather than pure, God uses the events in our lives to teach us and gift us with His character traits.

So, remember how you wanted something (or someone) so bad, you would do anything for it, and maybe you did. What happened after you got it? Did you lose interest in it? Did it lose interest in you? Did things fall apart around you or in your life? Did you lose valuable friendships or relationships? Did you lose your integrity? Did your reputation or credibility sink? These are all signs that what you got, wasn't assigned to you by God. When you endure and exercise the patience that God requires of you, the result isn't anything like what you read above. That's because the results above do not glorify God and our lives are meant to glorify Him.

The Word tells us that God places desires in our hearts. The hope or expectation being that we in turn come to Him about those desires asking for His counsel, guidance, and divine intervention. The complication we end up facing is this:

1) We get the God-given desire
2) We discuss it with God in prayer
3) He reveals a few steps, lines up some things and we get excited
4) Then God goes radio silent!

Um... hello, are you there? God, um, did you just change your number? Am I blocked? Did you block me? Suddenly your peers are celebrating their blessings on blessings on blessings, while you're trying to make sense of what is going on. Then you begin to question whether or not you even heard the voice of God. Whether or not He actually spoke something to you;

inspired you. Is this desire in fact from God? THIS is where that gift, that trait "patience" comes into play.

See, patience is that trait that causes you to sing different, smile different, rejoice different, praise different, and exemplify grace and compassion differently. Because being patient often means getting a lot of rejections or denials—feeling abandoned, forgotten, inadequate, and sometimes even crazy. The reason why we tend to feel these emotions isn't because we're weak-minded, but because we haven't experienced *this* testing of our faith. Let me be clear, whenever God gives you an idea, a desire, or calls on you to act on something, it won't always manifest or take place overnight. There are other people, places, and circumstances that must all align at His appointed time before we can see the result. Take heart, sis, because God's delay, is not His denial. We know that because He is not a liar. God is not a human being and therefore, won't tell you one thing and turn around and change His mind. If it doesn't happen, it's likely because YOU changed your mind.

When God goes silent after giving you this creative idea, that doesn't mean He gave up on you. No; it means that He is now making you earn it by getting you invested in Him on a deeper level. God wants a relationship with you. He wants that dream to materialize in your life. He wants others to see it materialize because that draws them to Him. But it only works if you remain faithful to Him and what He spoke to you about. That commitment is seen in the actions you take toward the dream He gave you. Just because God is silent does not mean you can't show Him that you believe what He said or revealed to you. And guess what? That proactive work you put in, trusting Him, is you demonstrating your faith in Him and reliance on Him.

Day 19

Once God decides the timing is right; your actions demonstrate that you believe; and all roads point to Him and only Him as being responsible for the outcome, it happens! The desire God placed in your heart, which you discussed with Him and took action on, He now makes a reality! That is promised to us in Psalms 37:4—take delight in the Lord and He will give you your heart's desires.

∾Additional Scriptures∾

2 Corinthians 6:6
Proverbs 10:22
Proverbs 25:15
Romans 8:24-25
Philippians 2:13

∾Prayer∾

Heavenly Father, I'm grateful you chose to inspire me with gifts, dreams, visions, and desires. I'm grateful that you exercised patience with me. Please forgive me for the times where I attempted and even did things on my own, for my own will and glory. Forgive me for trying to skip ahead and rush your process. Forgive me for not being patient with you or with those around me, as you have been with me. Help me. Help me to trust you faithfully and to serve you with a singleness of mind. When distractions arise to tempt me to speed up the process, or take shortcuts, reveal them to me and help me to turn away from those evil spirits. Show me clearly when a desire I have is not of your will or inspired by you and help me to reject those things in Jesus' name. I thank you again for your presence in my life and many gifts. May I be reminded of your promises and actively await your manifestations. In Jesus' name I pray, Amen.

Sister to Sister

Reflection of the Day: Remember, the teacher is always silent during the test; so, stay encouraged and keep persevering.

Day 20

∼Key Scripture∼

1 Thessalonians 5:5 📖 For you are all children of the light and of the day; we don't belong to darkness and night.

∼Discussion∼

Did you know that as a believer, you have light inside of you and that *you* are light? Well, while you may not know this to be true or remember it, the enemy certainly does. That's why he's quick to use your very own thoughts and even insecurities against you. Here's the deal, you've heard it before and I can't emphasize it enough, light conquers darkness. That means, as a believer, YOU can conquer darkness. But in a world that changes faster than the latest trend or challenge, we often allow ourselves to get lost in the shuffle of things, forgetting WHO we are and WHOSE we are. It makes sense though; with a culture that 'cancels' people for their morally sound beliefs, yet embraces those who lack integrity, it is easy to understand how believers wanting to be accepted and included in the world they live in, dim their light for the sake of pleasing others.

We've seen it before, perhaps in our own lives. The good news is that the damage done isn't irreparable. Once you are saved and accept the Lord Jesus as your personal savior, you become a child of light. Yes, during your journey on this earth, you may experience seasons where your light shines brighter than others. There may also be a period where your light isn't as bright. However, that light, regardless of how dim it may become is still present. If you're in that season of dimness, take courage because as long as you are alive, your light has not been extinguished, which means that it can grow brighter.

For those whose lights are shining bright, I encourage you to take inventory of your life. It's OK to do this and it is necessary as Luke 11:35 suggests we do this, telling us to "Make sure that the light you think you have is not actually darkness." Might seem confusing to say that all believers are light and yet their light may actually be darkness but when you dig a little deeper you understand the meaning of this verse. See, the person whose light is dim and the person whose light is shining bright both share a common denominator; their daily intake of the world around them.

The more you embrace the world, its ways and lifestyle trends, the more you find yourself initially trying to balance the world's needs with your very own spiritual needs. You bend a bit on your spiritual needs because 'no one will see' or 'no one will know' and 'I can get back to where I need to be, quickly.' Unfortunately, this compromise is usually the beginning of a bright light losing its strength. Habits don't form overnight. With the little give that you make here and there on the needs of your spiritual being, you begin to make room for the world's needs and start to make accommodations for its customs. But during this time, you still don't think of it as harmful, because you're saved and have a relationship with the Lord. To you, this is a good balance between living in the world and not being judgmental of those living in the world (outside of the Kingdom of God), while still living as a believer. I imagine that's why Jesus tells us in the scripture above to check

Day 20

ourselves. Because we can be so far-gone that we don't even realize that our light has become dim.

As believers in Christ, it's important that we fearlessly face the daily challenges from the enemy to dim our light. It's important that we remember that the light we carry isn't solely for us; it's for those around us who are in the dark. When you remember that you are light, you shine effortlessly, fearlessly, and boldly. You don't have to chase after things, they come to you. God's light within you will draw others to you. But you've got to trust Him. You have to be willing to bet on God with all that you have; ignore the culture around you and those living in darkness. Faith, integrity, morals, values, kindness, and compassion may not be in style right now, but they will all make a comeback. And guess who will be leading that comeback? YOU—the believer. Let God use His light within you to bring opportunities to you and to draw others to you. Those who are in darkness will see your light and seek after its source. But sis, you have to be unafraid to shine brightly. Remember, we radiate light. We carry the answer within us, and the answer is Jesus.

If you are surrounded by darkness, don't be afraid. Researchers from Texas A&M University have determined that without obstruction, the human eye can see a candle flame that is roughly 1.6 miles away. Imagine that! Your light is like this but better because it's God-given. You ever wonder how those in darkness are rarely afraid to express themselves but rather stand boldly in their ways, unafraid to challenge and be challenged? Yet, as believers, we tend to think we should assimilate for the greater good thought that's NOT what we're called to do.

We are called to be leaders and peacemakers. Darkness should be uncomfortable around light, not vice versa. So today, I'm going to challenge you to take some time and honestly reevaluate yourself. How do nonbelievers react to your presence? Are they comfortable being who they are or are you uncomfortable? Does your presence challenge them to be better, desire better or does it encourage them to remain lost in the darkness? Once you've done that, whatever the result is, talk to God about it. Make sure your heart is sincere and be prepared for the change and the challenges you'll face as a result of you wanting to improve and brighten your God-given light.

Live in love and walk in His light.

Additional Scriptures

Matthew 5:14
Matthew 5:16
Isaiah 60:3

Prayer

Dear God, thank you for your light! I admit there are times I've allowed my thoughts, insecurities, and society to influence how I live and glorify you. This has resulted in your light not shining as bright as it could or should; for that, I am sorry. Please forgive me for taking the light you gifted me with for granted. I'm grateful for this reminder of what you've given me and what I'm supposed to do with it. Help me to embrace your light so that the darkness that surrounds me will be cast out. Help me to serve you faithfully so that when others see me, they'll actually see your light. I pray that you will connect me with other children of light so that we can glorify you brightly. In the meantime, use me to graciously share your light with those who need it. I pray that as you draw opportunities and people to me, that you will be glorified

DAY 20

through it all. Thank you for doing this and so much more, in Jesus' name, Amen.

Reflection of the Day: Shine sis, SHINE!

Sister to Sister

Day 21
Freedom to Choose

~Key Scripture~

Romans 10:9-10 📖 If you openly declare that Jesus is Lord and believe in your heart that God raised him from the dead, you will be saved. For it is by believing in your heart that you are made right with God, and it is by openly declaring your faith that you are saved.

~Discussion~

Yes, I have the freedom to choose to believe in God and serve Him. While I do have that freedom, I understand that it didn't come without an expensive price. It's actually priceless. Now that I have chosen Him, I have to be all in. 1 Peter 1:15 says, "But now you must be holy in everything you do, just as God who chose you is holy." In all honesty, that's a hard request to fulfill but not an impossible one. Being holy requires a daily sacrifice of what our flesh wants, what the world and society tells us we should want, versus what the Holy Spirit wants. It doesn't mean I'm walking around meek or passive; rather, I'm walking in the authority of the God I believe in, through the power of His resurrected son, Jesus.

As followers of Christ, we believe that this earth that we currently occupy is our temporary home; meaning, we are foreigners. We are charged with living "in reverent fear of

Him" during our time as foreigners in this land. But wait, you may not know this because you are not a follower. That's OK, it's not too late to open your heart to the God of creation and receive His son Jesus as your Lord and Savior.

You know Jesus once said, "The world's sin is that it refuses to believe in me."

As we come to an end, I don't want to take for granted the humbling occasion I have to share the Lord's love with you. I don't want to assume that because you read this book, you already know Him as your personal Lord and Savior. Now that you've embedded yourself with the desire to read the Word and develop a deeper understanding of what it means to be a believer in this day and age, I invite you to join me in my heavenly home.

It doesn't matter how bad of a person you think you are or have been told you are. It also doesn't matter how good of a person you think you are or have been told you are. Sometimes "bad" people miss out on the FREE gift of salvation because they mistakenly allow themselves to believe the lie that they are beyond repair. Similarly, "good" people mistakenly deny themselves of this same gift because they believe that their deeds alone will save them. But save them from what? If you don't believe in Jesus, what would you need saving from? I tell you what; the way this world is these days, we could ALL use a savior! Maybe you're somewhere in the middle and just don't know. That's OK too, sis. It doesn't matter what version you identify as because TODAY, you have a unique opportunity to change the course of your future. Being good is cool but being saved is even better. Please know, just because a person is a do-gooder, that doesn't mean they have a heavenly place reserved for them in eternity. We are all sinners and no amount of good can erase that. Only the blood of Jesus can, and it already has. God won't force you to choose Him; He wants you to come to this decision on your own. He wants your heart, in its purest and sincerest form. That can only come through freewill. I hope you listen to His voice today and choose Him.

Additional Scriptures

John 16:9
Romans 3:23-24
John 14:6
Acts 4:12
Romans 8:29-30
Titus 3:4-7
Ephesians 2:8-9

Prayer

Dear God, thank you for allowing me to complete this devotional. Thank you for the ways in which you've spoken to me throughout the years and especially over these 21 days. Your Word says, you stand at the door and knock, and you ask me to not harden my heart. So right now, between me and you, I ask for your forgiveness of all my sins. I invite you into my heart and into my life, as Lord of my life. I believe that thousands of years ago, you sent your only son, Jesus, on this earth with the primary purpose of saving the souls of believers around the world, *if* they believe. I believe that the birth of Jesus was an unconditional act of love from you for which I can never repay you for. I believe His death, resurrection, and ascension into heaven solidifies His place in your presence and supremacy in all that is. Thank you, God, for being patient with me and for letting me live to see the day where I would choose you with all my heart, mind, body, and soul. Now, I invite you to come into my heart. Transform my thinking and bind those ways about me that dishonor you. I pray you will convict my spirit when the temptations of the world come to draw me away from you. Surround me with true believers and give me the discernment I need to make righteous decisions. Plant me in the right church where I will grow in my faith and be fearless in demonstrating your love. I thank you for doing all of this and more. Most importantly, I thank you for saving my soul. In Jesus' name I pray, Amen.

Reflection of the Day: Before you were born, you didn't get to choose who your parents or family members would be. But today, you can choose your eternal family for life in eternity. Welcome to the family of believers! I love you with the love of Christ.

Day 21

Sister to Sister

About The Author

Virginia was raised by her mother, Jeanette who instilled Christian values in her life at a young age. Like many believers, Virginia went through her seasons of tests and didn't always pass them. In 2016, she rededicated her life to the Lord and vowed to be used by Him for His glory. Sister to Sister is a labor of love and obedience, one for which she is grateful and humbled to share with you. Virginia is a licensed attorney and holds a master's degree in international affairs. When not working, Virginia can be found at home with family or friends, usually laughing and or singing. She enjoys volunteering, reading, listening to and composing music. Her 'superpower' is encouragement. Virginia currently resides in the DMV area and is a member of Alfred Street Baptist Church.